Dog Heroes

ABOUT THE COVER

Yoho, the friendly dog on the cover, is a malamute from Canada. This dog, just three years old and weighing ninety pounds when Jon Van Zyle painted his portrait, is as mellow and even-tempered as he is portrayed. He actually does smile when he's happy and he's happy most of the time.

Yoho was chosen as a model for *Dog Heroes* primarily because of his good looks, but he is a potential hero, too — as are many loyal and intelligent dogs who are protective of their human families.

When his mistress, Julie Coulson, went off to attend McGill University in Montreal, Yoho stayed home with her parents, Ann and D'Arcy Coulson, and quickly proved his worth. Walking with the young dog one cold, icy night near the Ottawa River, D'Arcy Coulson slipped, hitting his head on the ice, nearly knocking himself out. Yoho, who was trotting ahead, returned to check out the situation. When the dazed Coulson showed no will to rise, the dog became vocal, urging him on and, failing that, began to drag him toward their home. Coulson was so amazed that on another night, he pretended to be ill and, again, Yoho proved willing to drag him toward a safe place!

In 1995, when Julie traveled north to study at the University of Alaska Fairbanks, her parents sent Yoho to keep an eye on her.

The name "Yoho" translates to "awe and wonder" in the Blackfoot Indian language of the Rocky Mountain region where Julie Coulson first met her dog. Yoho's parents, Klondike and Nikiska, and his grandparents, Storm and Kiana, were well known in the area, and his mother was at one time the canine weight-pulling champion of British Columbia.

Dog Heroes

True Stories about Extraordinary Animals Around the World

Written by Tim Jones
Researched by Christine Ummel
Illustrated by Jon Van Zyle

Epicenter Press
Fairbanks/Seattle

Editor Christine Ummel has a feeling of *déjà vu* about the stories in this book. The text is based on extensive research she conducted in 1992 while participating in an eight-month student internship with Epicenter Press Inc. during her senior year at Seattle Pacific University. The internship helped Ummel land a job at Epicenter Press in Seattle, where she subsequently was promoted to associate editor and publicity coordinator. One of the first titles she saw through editing and design, three years after the internship that introduced her to book publishing, was *Dog Heroes*.

Project editor: Christine Ummel
Copy editor: Christine Ummel
Research: Christine Ummel, Dermot Cole
Cover and book design: Newman Design/Illustration
Prepress and printing: Color Magic, Inc.
Production and binding: Lincoln & Allen
Production manager: Dick Owsiany

Jones, Tim, 1942 –
    Dog heroes : true stories about extraordinary animals around the world / written by Tim Jones ; illustrated by Jon Van Zyle.
      p.   cm.
    Includes bibliographical references (p. 94, 95).
    ISBN 0-945397-22-4 (hardbound)
    1. Dogs—Anecdotes. 2. Animal heroes—Anecdotes. I. Van Zyle, Jon. II. Title.
SF416.J65   1995
636.7—dc20   95-30531
                                     CIP

To order single copies of DOG HEROES, mail $32.95 each (Washington residents add $2.70 sales tax) plus $5 for shipping to: Epicenter Press, Box 82368, Kenmore, WA 98028.

Booksellers: This book is available from major wholesalers. Retail discounts are available from our trade distributor, Graphic Arts Center Publishing Co., Box 10306, Portland, OR 97210. Phone 800-452-3032.

PRINTED IN THE UNITED STATES OF AMERICA

First printing, August, 1995

10 9 8 7 6 5 4 3 2 1

DOG HEROES

was written in the hope that
humans might better appreciate
their canine friends, and as a
tribute to those who ask
so little and give us so much.

To good dogs everywhere.

"The one absolutely

unselfish friend that a man

can have in this selfish world,

the one that never deserts him,

the one that never proves ungrateful

or treacherous, is his dog."

—U.S. Senator George Graham Vest,
"Eulogy of the Dog," Sept. 23, 1870

Dog Heroes

![paw] TABLE OF CONTENTS

8

FOREWORD

Years ago, while living among Alaska's Eskimos and Indians, I found the people bemused by the concept of dogs as house pets. Living off the land by subsistence hunting and fishing was so difficult that few could afford the luxury of a dog — unless that dog worked to earn its feed and care. Huskies were the main mode of transportation, and human lives often depended on them, just as the welfare of the dogs depended on the hunting success of the humans.

It was a harsh existence in which unusual bonds nonetheless were formed between dogs and humans. Once, in a poor Eskimo household, I was surprised to find the rare house pet — a crippled husky who, in her prime, had saved a member of the family from certain death by leading her through a severe storm. In gratitude, and at some hardship to themselves, the family had kept the dog beyond her days of usefulness.

One thing that puzzled me living in the high arctic was why dogs abandoned their free existence for a restrained life with humans when their wolf cousins still lived so naturally (and generally well) in the wilds. It was here, where their howls have the power to raise the hair on the nape of your neck, that I came to appreciate dogs' wonderful gift of companionship to humans.

Lael Morgan

Barry *Saint Bernard*

BARRY

igh in an Alpine pass between Switzerland and Italy stands a modest monastery. At 8,114 feet above sea level, it is one of the highest continually occupied places in Europe. Julius Caesar's legions climbed the pass on their way to conquer Gaul. The Romans built a stone road through it and a monument to their supreme deity, Jupiter, at the summit. This road became a popular route through the Alps, heavily used for centuries. Though records show that Hannibal brought his elephants by another way, there is some evidence that at least a portion of his army advanced through what has become known as "Great St. Bernard's Pass."

Sometime in the middle of the eleventh century, a young man named Bernard de Menthon renounced all earthly pleasures, including an impending marriage, and pledged his life to the church. As a monk, de Menthon traveled on this path through the Pennine Alps, where the snow often lies fifty feet deep and falls even through the summer.

> Over the centuries, Saint Bernards have saved thousands of travelers in the Pennine Alps.

Perhaps it was his own travails on the trail that inspired him. De Menthon received permission from Rome to establish a hospice in the pass to aid travelers as they hiked along the steep mountain path. He and his fellow monks from the Augustinian order established their monastery just below the summit and began a tradition of mountain rescue that would last for nine centuries.

De Menthon died in 1081, and the church canonized him as Saint Bernard in 1124. Soon afterward, his name was applied to the pass, the hospice, and later to a breed of dogs that would earn their reputation by carrying on the work begun by Saint Bernard.

The earliest written record of dogs saving a life in the pass dates to 1707, but a painting at the monastery dated 1695 shows the founder with a dog that looks much like the present-day Saint Bernard. Researchers estimate the dogs joined the monks in their work early in the 1600s. The lineage of the dogs has been traced variously to the Danish

13

Dog Heroes

bulldog, the mastiff of the neighboring Pyrenees Mountains, the Bernese mountain dog, and the Newfoundland. From all of these, perhaps, developed the large, splay-footed rescuer of mountain travelers. Originally it was known as the "Alpine dog," the "Alpine mastiff," or the "Hospice dog." The breed didn't receive its official name of "Saint Bernard" until 1882.

As a breed, these dogs are particularly suited to life in the mountains. Large-boned and strong, they have endless strength and stamina for plowing through the snow. The original Saint Bernards were bred to have short coats — dogs with longer coats were sold or given away, because snow caught in the long hairs would impede their progress in deep snow. The dogs' ability to work at high altitudes, along with their gentle natures, made them ideal for rescue work.

Saint Bernards probably were used first as guides for the monks. The dogs could find the trail in fog or whiteouts, even through a deep covering of snow. In those days all supplies for the monastery had to be carried there, after being bought in Aosta, Italy, to the south, or in Martigny, Switzerland, to the north. Monks bringing meat and milk from the Swiss, or wine and oil from the Italians, would be led through the snow to the monastery by one of their Saint Bernards.

As time passed, the dogs became not just guides, but rescuers. Perhaps a monk trapped by an avalanche was unexpectedly found by his guide dog. Saint Bernards have been known to yelp in the days before a volcanic eruption or earthquake, probably sensing the early tremors within the earth. This same sensitivity may lead them to a struggling victim buried in the snow of a sudden avalanche. It wasn't long before the Augustinians began training their Saint Bernards to locate and rescue mountaineers in distress.

The monks trained the dogs to work in pairs. Often the team of dogs would be sent out to patrol the upper reaches of the pass, or sometimes to find a lost traveler. When a male and a female together would locate a snowbound victim, the two of them would dig him out and perhaps lick him into consciousness. Then the female would lie down next to the person's body to warm it, while the male returned to its handlers to guide them to the scene. The instinct for this behavior remains in some members of the breed today.

The most famous of the dogs of the pass was a Saint Bernard named Barry. Born in 1800, the year Napoleon brought his army through the pass, Barry is credited with saving as many as forty people during the course of his life. His most famous deed was the rescue of a small boy.

The boy and his mother were making the long trek through the pass. At one of its steepest points, an avalanche thundered down the mountain, sweeping the two away in its fury. The child's mother did not survive. Barry found the boy, cold and unconscious, on the edge of a ravine so steep that none of the monks could reach him. The Saint Bernard descended the icy slope until he reached the child.

His first instinct was to lie down next to the boy to warm the little body. As he snuggled there, Barry began nudging the child and licking his face until consciousness returned. Somehow the dog induced the boy to grab onto him, holding on to his collar, a harness, or perhaps just his fur. Slowly Barry picked his way up the precipice, dragging the groggy boy through the snow. Finally they reached the waiting monks, who quickly took the boy to their monastery and cared for him until he was well again.

Today a monument commemorating Barry's most famous rescue stands in a French village. The statue depicts the child riding on the Saint Bernard's back; a plaque beneath the statue credits Barry with forty rescues, then states he was killed during his forty-first. That was a common fable — that Barry was attempting to revive a soldier when the confused man stabbed him, thinking he was being attacked by a wolf. The true story of Barry's death is more benign. In 1812, the monks retired an aging Barry from his mountain rescue work. They sent him to a family in Bern where he lived for two more years. Upon his death in 1814, Barry's remains were preserved and still stand in a Bern museum, a monument not just to Barry but to all the dogs of Great St. Bernard's Pass, whose efforts to date have saved more than 2,500 travelers in distress.

> *Saint Bernards aren't the only dogs that can climb mountains ...*

TSCHINGEL

One of the most famous mountain dogs of the 1800s was not a Saint Bernard, but a beagle. Swiss mountain guide Christian Almer purchased Tschingel as he passed through the village of Lotschthal in 1865. He'd bought the large, female beagle as a watchdog, but after a disappointing climb with client W.A.B. Coolidge in 1868, he gave Coolidge the dog to cheer him up. From that time on, Coolidge and Tschingel were inseparable in the mountains. During their first climb together, the beagle reached the summit of 12,044-foot Blumlisalphorn. Tschingel became particularly adept at recognizing crevasses in glaciers and could lead climbers away from dangerous routes. Her greatest accomplishment was the ascension of Mount Blanc in 1875. Tschingel ran ahead of the climbing party, the first to make it to the top and the first dog to reach the 15,782-foot summit on her feet (apparently a couple of dogs had been carried to the top before her). During their nine years of climbing together, Coolidge and Tschingel climbed almost every noteworthy peak in the Alps, a total of sixty-six major climbs.

16

Greyfriars Bobby *Skye terrier*

GREYFRIARS BOBBY

Sometime in the mid-1850s, a Skye terrier came to live on a farm in the Pentland Hills southwest of Edinburgh, Scotland. Named Bobby, the little dog attached himself to John Grey, the farmer's shepherd. John Grey, called "Auld Jock" by his friends, was a fixture in those Scottish hills. Jock and Bobby became inseparable, tending the farmer's sheep and traveling once a week to market in the capital. Market Day always featured a special lunch at the Greyfriars Dining Rooms. When the Edinburgh Castle gun sounded at 1 p.m., Jock and Bobby left whatever they were doing and headed for the dining room where they shared their meal ... sometimes over the protests of the manager.

Within a couple of years after meeting Bobby, Jock's age began to weigh on him, and he contracted tuberculosis. He headed into retirement, taking small quarters in Edinburgh. Forced to leave Bobby at the farm, Jock moved to the capital alone, but he wasn't alone for long. The day after Jock left, Bobby escaped from the farm. When Jock showed up at the Greyfriars Dining Rooms at the sound of the one o'clock gun, Bobby rushed in to join him. Reunited, the two friends enjoyed their lunch, then returned to Jock's rooms where the old man made plans to return the little terrier to the farm on the next Market Day.

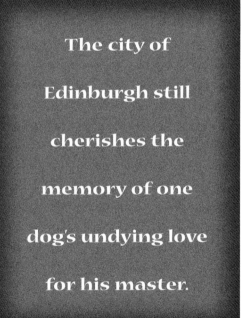

The city of Edinburgh still cherishes the memory of one dog's undying love for his master.

It was never to be. Before he could return Bobby, Jock's tuberculosis overtook him and he died. Two days later neighbors found Bobby guarding the body, at first not allowing anyone to come near. Jock's few friends arranged a simple funeral. As the procession moved through the streets of Edinburgh, Bobby tagged along, following the casket containing his friend to Greyfriars Cemetery. The cemetery used for the royalty of Scotland was also the final resting place for Auld Jock. Such revered ground wasn't for the convenience of dogs, however. When the funeral service ended and the mourners departed, the sexton spotted Bobby lying near his friend's half-filled grave. He chased Bobby from the hallowed ground, but as soon as the sky turned dark, Bobby sneaked back to the grave and spent the night there.

In the morning the sexton, who was named James Brown, chased him from the cemetery again, but that night Bobby returned. Soon the little dog found a daytime hiding place beneath a fallen tombstone, where he could spend his days undetected as he kept his vigil. In time Bobby's persistence won the sexton over and, though it meant breaking the cemetery's rules, Brown allowed Bobby to stay near the grave. He even taught Bobby to hide on Sundays, when the churchyard had its largest number of visitors. For one of the church's high-ranking patrons, to have a dog in the cemetery would have been next to blasphemy.

For a couple of weeks Bobby kept his watch, ignoring even his own needs. Then one day, at the sound of the castle gun, he showed up at the Greyfriars Dining Rooms for lunch. The proprietor, a man named John Traill, recognized him as Auld Jock's dog and fed him. From that day forward, Bobby arrived at the inn every day at one o'clock, to be fed by Traill or whoever else was managing the inn at the time.

Once he'd gained the sexton's friendship and found a way to get regular meals, Bobby lived by the grave of the shepherd unhindered until 1867, when the city began to round up all unlicensed dogs. Dogcatchers nabbed Bobby and took him to Edinburgh's version of the pound. When the terrier failed to answer the one o'clock gun one day, John

Traill guessed what had happened. He rescued Bobby from being destroyed by telling the story of the faithful little dog to the city's Burgher Court. Traill's plea brought Bobby instant fame, and none other than the Lord Provost of Edinburgh paid for the dog's license. The Lord Provost, Sir William Chambers, even ordered a collar made with an inscription that read, "Greyfriars Bobby. From Lord Provost. 1867. Licensed."

Sporting his new collar, Bobby had the run of the city. Still, he held to his routine, guarding his master's grave and dropping by for lunch at the Greyfriars every day at one. Bobby's fame and popularity spread until he no longer had to hide from visitors — in fact, many visitors came to the cemetery specifically to see him. More than one artist painted the dog's portrait as he sat near Auld Jock's grave.

In 1872, after maintaining his vigil over Auld Jock's grave for fourteen years, Bobby's heart gave out and he died in the cemetery. The city mourned his death. Yet his burial site was a secret for some time. If the church wouldn't let dogs visit the cemetery, how could it allow a dog to be buried there? Nevertheless, the sexton dug Bobby a small grave near Jock's, then marked it with only a rosebush.

Upon learning about the inspiring little dog, the Baroness Burdett-Coutts asked to build a monument to the two inseparable friends. The church refused her request. Not to be denied, the baroness commissioned a work to stand outside the churchyard gates. City officials unveiled the monument a year after Bobby's death. As part of the monument, water from bubbling fountains poured into two basins; on top, a bronze likeness of Bobby faced longingly toward the gates of the cemetery.

In the years that followed, various authors told and retold the story of Bobby's vigil. Knowledge about him spread worldwide. Today, in the Greyfriars Dining Rooms, a plaque marks the spot where Bobby took his meals. The city's Huntly Museum proudly displays the collar given him by Sir William and the feeding dish he used at the inn. Filmmakers have produced two movies about his life, one starring a Skye terrier, the other featuring none other than Lassie. At last, in the early 1930s, the church allowed American donors to erect a small stone in the Greyfriars Cemetery, marking the grave of Auld Jock and the dog who loved him, Greyfriars Bobby.

He was a dog of legendary faithfulness ...

VIGE

Around 1000 AD, King Olaf I of Norway embraced Christianity and set about converting the rest of his known world. During his invasion of Ireland, his men went ashore, ordered to round up all the cattle they could find for food. As the Viking warriors drove the great herds of cattle toward the seashore, an Irish farmer came to Olaf, asking that his twenty cows be spared, as they were his only livelihood. Olaf, amused, told the man that if he could find his twenty cows from among the thousands, he could keep them. With that, the farmer whistled up his Irish wolfhound, named Vige, and set him to work. Within minutes Vige had separated the farmer's twenty cows from the giant herd. Impressed, Olaf allowed the farmer to keep his cattle but asked to buy the dog. The farmer gave Vige as a gift to the king. From then on, through many battles, Vige remained at the king's side. It's said that, after Olaf fought and defeated one of his most fearsome enemies, Vige ran after the fleeing man and captured him. Later, in his final battle, Olaf was driven overboard and drowned by his enemies from Denmark and Sweden. Vige, learning his master had died, swam to shore, climbed to an overlook, and stayed there without food or water until he, too, died.

20

Owney *Mongrel*

OWNEY

Picture the Albany, New York, post office on a late night in the fall of 1888. The plain walls of the post office surround the clerks sorting the next day's mail, wearing their sleeves in garters and green celluloid shades to protect their eyes from the glare of the gas lights. One of the men walks outside to bring in more of the big canvas bags of mail that have come off the train from New York City. Through a door left open for a moment comes the scruffiest-looking little terrier anyone could imagine. According to legend, the dog sneaked onto a pile of mailbags and fell asleep. The postmen didn't notice him until morning. When they did, a friendly wag of his tail won the dog a family for life. Soon he was eating from the clerks' lunch pails and sleeping on their mailbags, taking to the mailman's life like a letter to an envelope.

Once adopted by the postal workers, "Owney" was given a name (reportedly taken from a slurring of one of his friends' names) and settled into a life of comfort at the post office. However, the wanderlust

Adopted by a post office in 1888, this little mongrel loved traveling with the U.S. mail.

that first led him there still coursed through him. One day he followed one of the delivery men along his route. When that didn't satisfy his itchy feet, he followed the mailbags to the railway station and boarded the train right along with the mail. On that, his first trip along the tracks, Owney made a round trip to New York City, returning to Albany a few days later. It was the start of a lifetime of traveling that would eventually take him around the world.

The friendly little mongrel made a habit of boarding trains with the mail and traveling across the country, always somehow finding his way back to Albany. When his benefactors began to worry that their pet might not return one day, they had a tag made that read simply "Owney, Post Office, Albany, New York." Sporting his new jewelry, Owney rode the rails wherever he chose. According to accounts from his traveling companions, and to the few photographs of him that survive, Owney enjoyed his train rides either lying on a pile of mailbags or sticking his face out the door of the mail

21

car, looking out at the scenery.

All across the country, postal workers Owney visited took to attaching baggage tags to his collar to mark his travels. Every time Owney returned to Albany, he carried home a new collection of jewelry, souvenirs of visits to post offices in most of the states of the Union. Owney didn't limit himself to post offices. He also brought back mementos from a Republican convention, a bankers' association meeting, a poultry producers' convention, and the Produce Exchange in Toledo, Ohio. Some people gave him tokens entitling him to a loaf of bread or a quart of milk. Occasionally Owney showed up at dog shows and brought back prizes for being the "Most Traveled Dog" or "Globetrotter."

In time the medals became too burdensome for the small dog and his small collar. But Owney didn't take his problem to just anyone. He followed the mailbags to Washington, DC, where none other than the Postmaster General of the United States, John Wanamaker, fitted him with a harness-like jacket to help him carry his souvenirs. In all, Owney collected 1,017 medals and tags documenting his adventures.

The artificial boundaries of states and countries meant little to a traveler like Owney. Reportedly he went to Mexico and to Canada; his friends from Albany had to bail him out of confinement in Montreal when postal workers there demanded payment for his keep. But when he embarked on his greatest trip of all, Owney showed that even oceans couldn't confine the wanderlust of a mail car dog.

Returning from a trip to Alaska (not a mean feat in itself), Owney showed up in a post office in Tacoma, Washington. From there the little dog walked up the gangplank of the steamship *Victoria* where he was taken in as the guest of Captain Panton on August 19, 1895. First stop: Yokohama. When the Japanese potentates of the Mikado saw Owney with his jacket of medals, they assumed that he was the property of a very important person. As a result, Owney traveled unhindered through Japan under the personal seal of the emperor. But the lure of the mail called, so Owney moved on to Foochow in China. His travels took him back to Japan, then on to Hong Kong, where he received a personal passport from the Chinese emperor. From Hong Kong, Owney began his return voyage westward, picking up tags in Singapore, Suez, Algiers, and the Azores before arriving in New York aboard the *Port Phillip*.

Word had preceded his arrival, and a crowd gathered to greet Owney when he came down the gangplank. Postal workers, recognizing the dog's chance for some kind of record, quickly relayed Owney across the country from mail car to mail car until he arrived back in Tacoma on December 29, 1895, completing his voyage around the world in 132 days. Including his trip around the globe, Owney is credited with traveling 143,000 miles throughout his career.

Toward 1897, Owney began to show signs of getting old. It was impossible to tell for sure, because no exact record of his age existed. Some reports claimed he was as much as ten years old when he entered the Albany Post Office in 1888; others said he was only a pup then. Nonetheless, nine years later, Owney had lost his sight in one eye, survived on soft foods, and had developed a bit of an attitude. The clerks in Albany tried to keep him at home, but Owney would have none of it. One day he slipped out of the post office and boarded a train. The last of his journeys took him back to Toledo, Ohio. There it seems that Owney was introduced to a newspaper reporter and the encounter somehow turned nasty. In whatever scuffle ensued, Owney received a fatal gunshot wound and died in Toledo on June 11, 1897.

Postal workers across the country lost a friend that day. Owney's body was sent to a taxidermist and the mount, along with all of his medals and tags, eventually ended up with the Postal Museum, part of the Smithsonian collection. Those clerks riding the rail cars must have felt a special loss at the death of Owney. In the days of the late nineteenth century, train wrecks were common; 400 were reported in 1893. A wreck often meant injury to the postal workers because their car usually was right behind the engine's tender. In his nine-year career riding the rails with the U.S. mail, however, no train with Owney on board ever wrecked or injured the mail clerks.

Taking a trip cross-country? Your dog might be a valuable companion ...

SCANNON

Credited as a valuable member of the expedition, a Newfoundland named Scannon crossed the continent with Lewis and Clark from 1804 to 1806. President Thomas Jefferson had charged the two with exploring the Louisiana Purchase. Their expedition took them over the Great Plains and Rocky Mountains to the shores of the Pacific Ocean. Scannon went every step of the way. Reports from Meriwether Lewis's journals say the dog quickly learned to hunt ducks and geese, bringing them back to the explorers' table. One report had him turning the charge of a buffalo that threatened his master. Sometimes grizzly bears bothered the camps, and Scannon proved adept at discouraging their nocturnal visits. The Newfoundland proved so valuable that when a group of Native Americans kidnapped him in the Columbia River Valley, Lewis sent three men to the rescue. The kidnappers, seeing the men in pursuit, released the dog and he returned to the expedition. 🐾

23

24

Nick Carter *Bloodhound*

NICK CARTER

The ability of hounds to follow a scent has raised a thousand legends since they appeared on the scene, perhaps before the time of Christ. Several breeds have evolved, but the champion tracker of all time, particularly for following a human scent, is the bloodhound. Some archeological findings show their use beginning in the early Middle East; others indicate that the citizens of the Roman Empire used them in the hunt. Better records have them raised by monks in western France and brought to Great Britain by the Norman conquerors.

By that time the breed had picked up its rather fearsome-sounding name of "bloodhound." One theory has it that traditionally these dogs were owned by the nobility, the "blue bloods," so the dogs were called "bloodhounds," the hounds belonging to the blood. Other theories relate the name to the dogs' ability to follow a blood trail. But the notion that the name comes from the animals' "bloodthirsty" nature is laughable

This Kentucky bloodhound tracked down more than 650 criminals and countless missing persons.

— the only danger a bloodhound's victim faces is drowning in slobber from being licked.

The friendliness of bloodhounds is one of the attributes that makes them useful in the pursuit of humans. Handlers don't have to worry about the dogs hurting their human targets; in fact, working bloodhounds must be kept on leashes because they have been known to locate their objectives, befriend them, and run off with them. Also, it helps that bloodhounds work quietly, rarely barking. That way they don't warn the pursued that a dog is on his trail.

Of course, the bloodhound's biggest asset is its highly evolved sense of smell. In the human nose, the cellular structure that enables you to smell, the olfactory membrane, would cover a little over one square inch. In its long snout with its haughty Roman hump, however, a bloodhound may have as many as fifty-nine square inches of olfactory membrane, spread along scrolls of paper-thin bone and in hair-

Dog Heroes

like cilia. Scientists estimate that a bloodhound's sense of smell is somewhere between 300,000 and three million times as powerful as that of a human being.

These expert sniffers were brought to the United States shortly after the Civil War. One of the most famous bloodhounds in American history was a black and tan fellow named Nick Carter, born in 1899. His owner was Volney Mullikin, the police chief in Lexington, Kentucky. Mullikin used bloodhounds in his police work, eventually buying a kennel so he could raise and train them. As his career progressed, Mullikin and his dogs traveled all over the middle and southeastern states to track down criminals and lost children. Nick Carter was his prize, his dog with the biggest reputation. In his time, Nick set a record by following a trail that was 105 hours old, tracking down an arsonist who had burned a farmer's outbuilding.

The weather must have been damp for the previous few days as Captain Mullikin led Nick to the charred remains of the farmer's henhouse, which had been burned to its baseboards more than four days before. Dampness helps bloodhounds follow a trail because it adheres particles of scent to the ground or nearby shrubbery. In dry weather, the scent blows away and spreads, making the trail more difficult to locate.

In spite of all of the distracting odors of burned wood and the many people who had walked around the area recently, Nick was able to pick out the culprit's scent. After a period of snuffling around the

site, the dog headed off into the woods, moving almost silently. Nick followed the scent, dragging the captain after him for more than a mile. Then the bloodhound approached a house. Hearing some noise outside, a man opened the door. Immediately Nick went to him, probably wagging his tail and attempting to lick whatever part of the man he could reach.

Captain Mullikin, who was accomplished in the art of drawing a suspect into an admission of guilt, quickly asked, "You weren't counting on the hounds when you burned the henhouse, were you?"

The surprised suspect simply answered, "No," admitting his guilt to Captain Mullikin and confirming Nick's identification of him as the arsonist.

Throughout his career, Nick received credit for more than 650 identifications resulting in convictions. During a one-year period, as reported in the *Lexington (Kentucky) Herald* in 1903, Nick Carter was responsible for 126 convictions, failing in only thirty-five cases. And those numbers don't begin to include all the people Nick located over the years. No one knows how many lost children or injured persons Nick found, but a few stories remain.

In one case, Mullikin was asked to help locate a little girl who had been last seen playing with her pet dog near a river. When evening fell, the dog returned home without the child. Neighbors searched in vain through the night and into the next day. In the morning they began dragging the river for the child's body.

Captain Mullikin brought Nick Carter to

the scene twenty-seven hours after the girl's disappearance had been reported. The girl's father offered Mullikin an article of his daughter's clothing, which Mullikin presented to Nick. The two men followed the dog to the riverbank where the child had last been seen.

Nick immediately turned from the river, dragging Mullikin with him into the woods. The father stumbled after them, lighting the way with a gas lantern. With the bloodhound tugging them along, the two men tripped over roots and ducked tree branches. Along one treacherous pathway, both men tripped over some obstruction and the lantern fell to the ground, shattering and extinguishing their light. Nick only pulled all the harder while the girl's father struck matches to illuminate the dark woods.

The rush through the brush stopped as quickly as it had started. As the men caught their breath, and a match died, from the silence of the woods came a child's cooing sound. One of the men struck another match. In the small circle of light they saw the man's daughter, her clothing held fast in a tangle of brambles. She had one arm around Nick Carter's wrinkled neck as the dog happily licked her face.

DOX

Sometimes the best detective on the case is a dog ...

If one breed of dog has excelled in police work, it's the German shepherd. And of all the German shepherds who have worked with policemen, one of the most successful was owned and handled by an Italian police officer, Giovanni Maimone. He and his dog, Dox, together solved dozens of cases in the 1940s and 1950s in cities throughout Italy. By 1957, as part of the "Flying Squad" of the Rome police, Dox was named a corporal and given a monthly wage. In one of his most amazing cases, Dox was called in to investigate a jewelry store burglary in which a guard had wrestled with the intruder. Dox tracked the burglar to his apartment, but the man claimed he'd been asleep and the guard couldn't make a positive identification. Maimone took the dog back to the store, where Dox sniffed around, then found a loose button and dropped it in front of his master. Then he led the police again to the suspect's dwelling. There Dox sniffed out an overcoat— one button was missing and the others matched the one Dox had found in the jewelry store. The culprit confessed. At the time of his death at age nineteen in 1965, Dox was credited as responsible for at least 400 arrests.

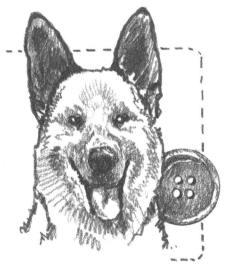

Rags *Terrier*

RAGS

When a little dog called Rags showed up at the Long Island Kennel Club Dog Show in 1925 and officials demanded a pedigree, not even the dog's handlers could tell them exactly what he was. As venerable a reporter as the *New York Times* called him a Scottish-Irish terrier. So Rags didn't get into the show. But when the club learned of the dog's history, it not only let him enter the next year, but also established a special category just for him. Rags took home the "War Dog Sweepstakes Championship."

For what Rags lacked in pedigree, he made up for with courage, intelligence, and loyalty. According to published accounts, sometime during World War I, Army Private Jimmy Donovan snuck away from his unit to enjoy the thrills of Paris. The air raid sirens went off, the city went dark, and Donovan, stumbling through the blacked-out unknown territory, bumped into a scraggly, olive-gray dog. Donovan picked up the dog just before he ran into the military police. The private was away from his unit without leave at the time and, on demand from the MPs, told them he'd been out searching for the unit's mascot. Told the dog looked like a pile of rags, Donovan retorted that was, indeed, the dog's name. The military police then allowed the private to return to his unit with the new "First Division mascot."

Donovan served in the Signal Corps, stringing communications wires between units to carry messages directing placements, troop movements, and artillery fire. Rags went everywhere with Donovan and quickly learned to be useful. Incoming artillery shells made a distinct sound, and Rags picked up on the sound and the fact that all the men dove to the ground when they heard it. With his acute hearing, Rags could hear the shells coming long before his human comrades, and as soon as he did, he'd squash his belly into the dirt. His fellow soldiers learned to read his actions and hit the dirt on his signal.

> Adopted by an American private during World War I, Rags ran vital messages for the U.S. Signal Corps.

Dog Heroes

By the end of their first month together, Donovan had taught Rags to carry a message between himself and his headquarters. Donovan's first assignment after finding Rags was to maintain the communications lines between advancing infantry and artillery during the battle for Soissons, about one hundred miles northwest of Paris. While a unit fought for control of the road between Paris and Soissons, Donovan found himself desperately trying to repair the lines connected to the front. Command was attempting to find a unit with which it had lost contact. As Donovan worked, Rags trotted up with a note in his mouth. The note gave the missing unit's position, and Donovan passed it on to headquarters. Later he learned the messenger had been killed while attempting to crawl through the hostile fire.

Donovan went with the front-line infantry as it drove toward Germany, along the way earning a promotion to sergeant. Though he was a communications expert, when a squad leader died, Donovan took command. As the unit crawled through the barbed wire and trenches on the battlefield, they chanced upon a German patrol. The Germans attacked, one of them directly at Donovan. Rags jumped to the defense, snapping and biting at the enemy's feet, distracting him long enough for Donovan to get the upper hand. Later, in another battle, a German knocked Donovan down. The enemy soldier was reaching for his pistol when Rags bit his hand, forcing him to drop the gun and giving the sergeant the precious seconds necessary to recover and escape.

Donovan and Rags followed the front across France, Donovan patching the communications wires when he could and, when he couldn't, sending Rags with messages. The push stopped at the Argonne Forest. There the Germans had concentrated their forces for a major defense, and the advancing Allied forces encountered some of the worst fighting in the whole war.

Pinned down by enemy fire, Donovan worried because his own force's guns were silent. He tapped into a line and learned a strategic hill had been taken by the Allies but they needed artillery support to hold it. Understanding the importance of the message, Donovan crept from his hole and began tracing wires to find where they had broken between him and the artillery. Rags ran ahead, trying to help by barking when he came to a break in the wire, but was hindered by the gas mask he had to wear. When Donovan realized he couldn't repair the wire, he wrote a note, identifying the hill and the situation, and tied it to Rags's collar. Just as the dog was about to leave, a shell hit nearby. Fragments tore off both their gas masks. A shard of shrapnel mangled the dog's right eye and another tore into his foreleg. With the deadly gas choking them, Donovan gave the note to Rags, who took it in his mouth and staggered off toward the artillery a little less than two miles away. After a few minutes, another shell knocked Rags down, rolling him into a foxhole. A soldier in the hole read the note, then picked up the dog and ran toward the battalion artillery. There the officers, once alerted to the situation, began bombarding the hill, turning back the attacking Germans. As they did, a group of soldiers brought in the wounded Donovan, who also had been hit a second time.

Medics sent dog and man to a field hospital, then to a rear echelon recovery facility. As days passed, Rags recovered, but he would spend the rest of his life with a limp, one blind eye, and a slight cough. Donovan didn't recover as well; the gas had almost paralyzed his lungs. Doctors sent him back to the United States. Along the way, orderlies and officers bent various rules to allow Rags to go with his master. Eventually the two friends arrived at Fort Sheridan, near Chicago, where soldiers took care of Rags and sometimes allowed him into the hospital to see Donovan. In time Donovan's lungs simply gave out, and Rags arrived one morning to find an empty bed. After a period of mourning in which he lay sadly by his master's bed, Rags recovered and became the mascot of the entire base. When Major R.W. Hardenbergh arrived at the base, his family adopted the dog and from then on Rags traveled to the various stations where Major Hardenbergh was assigned. Rags died at the age of twenty, having received numerous commendations and awards from military and civilian organizations.

The poodle who went into battle with Napoleon's troops ...

MOUSTACHE

The Emperor Napoleon had a long history with dogs and valued their abilities. One dog that caught his attention was a large poodle that joined a regimental parade in Paris and followed the troops on Napoleon's Italian campaign.

"Moustache" received a grenadier's rations and station, along with a weekly combing and trim for his fine, mustache-like whiskers. At the battle for Marengo, Moustache recognized a spy. A courier had entered a French encampment and was riding through it unsuspected, noting troop strength and positioning. That is, until he ran into Moustache. The dog bristled, snarled, and started barking at the horseman. French troops accosted the man and quickly learned he was an Austrian gathering information for his own army. One story claims that Moustache grabbed the flag from a fallen standard-bearer and, dodging bayonet thrusts, brought the flag safely to his own lines. Accompanying the troops into the heavy fighting in Spain, Moustache was killed by a cannonball. His comrades-in-arms gave him a full military funeral. 🐾

32

Tang *Newfoundland*

TANG

The friendliness of the giant Newfoundland can be traced through its centuries-old partnership with man. As with many breeds, time has muddied the history of the Newfoundland. They have been traced variously to the Great Pyrenees dogs and to Norwegian sailors who may have brought the dogs to the New World. The most likely history places the Newfoundland in North America long before European contact. Once the dogs roamed wild, from the East Coast to the Great Plains, from Saskatchewan to Mexico. First domesticated by the Algonquins and later by the Sioux, the dogs served as beasts of burden and hunting companions for centuries until the Spanish brought the horse to North America. The name of the breed came from the country where Europeans first encountered them, the island province of Newfoundland off the coast of eastern Canada.

The first European settlers on the island, and the mariners who supplied them, soon discovered the value of these large dogs, who weighed an average of 150 pounds, had long legs with webbed feet, and seemed naturally devoted to human masters. Soon Newfoundlands were hauling carts full of firewood from the forests; helping fishermen drag their heavy nets ashore; and, once it became clear they were talented swimmers and lifesavers, joining the men at sea.

As trade grew along the coast and across the oceans, many ships carried a Newfoundland on board. The dogs were excellent swimmers and natural-born retrievers, so little training was necessary to teach them to dive into the water after equipment or people that had been washed overboard. A drowning sailor would find a Newfoundland suddenly beside him, gripping his clothing in its teeth or maybe just offering its strong back for him to hang onto, as together they struggled back to the ship.

> The lives of ninety-two people, trapped on the wrecked steamship *Ethie*, depended on one brave Newfoundland.

Dog Heroes

Loyal companions, the dogs were highly valued for their lifesaving abilities. Often they were the first to indicate a landfall, their sensitive noses picking up the scent of shore among the sea breezes. Mostly Newfoundlands traveled with the fishermen exploring the Grand Banks fishing grounds off the coast of Canada, but many traveled the globe even as late as the time of the clipper ships.

The most famous rescue by a Newfoundland came in 1919, when the coastal steamer *Ethie* foundered off the coast of the dogs' namesake island.

Winter storms in the North Atlantic generate not only raging winds and mountainous seas but also driving, blinding snow to complicate the mariner's voyage. Along the rocky coast of the Canadian Maritimes, spires reach up through the water to rip out the bottom of any unfortunate vessels caught near the shore.

In December of 1919, the *Ethie* fought a snowstorm within a gale until she came into the surf close to Martin's Point in Bonne Bay on the coast of Newfoundland. With over ninety people aboard, the steamship went aground on the rocks off shore and lay at the mercy of the pounding waves. Rockets fired by the crew alerted people ashore, who came to the beach to help with the rescue. What they needed was a connection, some way to move the passengers and crew safely from the ship to the shore.

The crew attempted to shoot one of the ship's lines to the people on the beach, but it fell short. Then a sailor took a rope and jumped into the surf, attempting to swim the lifeline to the beach. Waves swept him away, and he was never seen again. The passengers and crew aboard the *Ethie* stood so near to shore, yet so far.

That's when the ship's Newfoundland, Tang, caught the attention of the captain. One has to wonder what the captain thought. Perhaps he'd heard stories about Newfoundlands but never actually had seen one perform. He was running out of choices. The captain ordered the crew to retrieve the lifeline and give the end to Tang. Taking the line in his teeth, the dog plunged into the surf and headed toward shore.

In those gale-driven waters, Tang must have struggled, the waves pounding against him, the undertow trying to drag him out to sea. He swam on, shaking the salt water out of his eyes, until he approached the beach. Some of the rescue party waded into the surf and reached the dog. They took the line from his mouth and fastened it to a strong point. With the connection made, the ship's crew quickly rigged up a system of ropes and pulleys and attached to it a "breeches buoy," a seat made out of a pair of short pants hanging inside a round life preserver. One by one, sitting inside the breeches buoy, ninety-one people aboard the *Ethie* were shuttled over the waves to the shore.

An infant presented a problem. If the baby's mother carried him in her arms, then was dipped into the surf, the child might be torn away by the strength of the waves. Instead, creative sailors fixed a mailbag to the lifeline and put the baby inside. Safe in his bag, the baby was pulled along the lifeline to the waiting hands of his rescuers.

History doesn't record what Tang did once he'd made his way to shore, but it's not hard to picture the excited dog searching for his master, greeting every passenger that descended from the breeches buoy. Lloyd's of London, the famous insurance agency, later awarded the brave dog with a medal for Meritorious Service, which he wore on his collar for the rest of his life.

The *New York Times* reported the rescue a week later, citing communications difficulties because the storm had knocked down all power and communications lines. In the article, Tang was credited with saving ninety-two lives, perhaps the largest number of lives saved by any dog in a single incident.

SINBAD

A s mascot of the Coast Guard ship *Campbell* during World War II, Sinbad lived the life of a sailor. A seaman first found the mutt inebriated with his muzzle in the gutter. When the *Campbell*'s captain discovered the dog on board his ship, he intended to drop him off at the next port of call, but by the time they arrived, Sinbad had charmed both the crew and the officers. Soon Sinbad was listed in the personnel files, had his own bunk, and would yip when his name was shouted at the morning "muster," or role call. He also demonstrated some of the vices of the stereotypical sailor. At least once during his career he was busted from "Chief Dog" to "First Class Dog" after a bout with whiskey and beer at a party near the Brooklyn Navy Yard. But if he was there in the revelries, he was also there in battle. Once the *Campbell* took on six German U-boats, sinking the last by ramming it — which left the cutter without power, its engine room flooded, drifting for more than three days. Through it all, Sinbad remained on deck with his comrades. He served aboard the Campbell from 1937 until he retired in 1948. When veterans of the ship gathered in 1986 to remember their mascot, the one universal memory was this: in all the battles they fought with Sinbad on board, not one sailor was killed.

The ups and downs of life as an official ship's dog ...

35

36

Buddy *German shepherd*

BUDDY

The idea of guide dogs for the blind has been around for centuries. Drawings from as early as 100 BC show blind people being led by dogs, and the use of guide dogs continued through the Middle Ages into modern times. However, for the most part, guide dogs were associated with misery and poverty. Several sixteenth century paintings, for example, depict beggars being led by dogs on leashes. It wasn't until after World War I that guide dogs helped the blind on a regular basis, and that was only in Europe, particularly Germany, where the large number of blind war veterans overwhelmed the number of human guides available to help them.

So while guide dogs became fairly commonplace in Germany in the 1920s and 1930s, American associations for the blind dismissed the idea. The head of one prestigious school for the blind described the guide dog as "a dirty little cur dragging a blind man along at the end of a string, the very index of incompetence and beggary."

> The first Seeing Eye dog in the U.S., Buddy helped thousands of blind Americans become more independent.

It took three people and a German shepherd named Buddy to bring guide dogs across the Atlantic. The first of these people was an American woman named Dorothy Eustis. From a background in breeding cattle, Eustis began experimenting with dogs and their intelligence. She moved to Europe in 1923 and, at a chalet in the Swiss Alps, began raising and training German shepherds in a place she called "Fortunate Fields." She and her chief trainer, Jack Humphrey, trained dogs to work with the police, the Red Cross, and the army.

Eventually word of their work reached back to the United States, and an editor of the *Saturday Evening Post* asked Eustis to write a story about her dogs. One of the reasons Eustis had left the U.S., however, was because she thought Americans breeding German shepherds for show were destroying the dogs' natural intelligence and working abilities. Eustis worried that creating a reputation for her working dogs would bring American show breeders to her door wanting to buy the dogs. So, instead of writing about her own working dogs, she chose to write about a school in Potsdam, Germany, where dogs were being trained to guide the blind. Eustis titled her article "The Seeing Eye."

The article brought hundreds of responses from blind people in the United States. One that struck her was from Morris Frank, a nineteen-year-old blind man who lived in Nashville, Tennessee. Frank had grown up helping his blind mother until accidents took first one, then the other of his own eyes. At the time he wrote the letter, Frank already had been battling for freedom, refusing to accept his society's assumption that a blind man was only good for pushing brooms as a janitor. Instead Frank taught himself to read Braille and enrolled at Vanderbilt University, pursuing a career in the growing insurance industry.

Eustis and Humphrey decided Morris Frank would be the ideal person to introduce guide dogs to the United States. Eustis wrote back to him, asking him to come to Fortunate Fields and be taught how to use a guide dog. Frank's trip to Switzerland was itself an example of how desperately blind people needed some way to get around independently. Not knowing how else to move a blind person across the ocean and then across Europe, an American Express clerk sent Frank as a package. He was escorted, shut in his cabin, left to sit, and not allowed to move about until his last escort delivered him to the train platform in Vevey, Switzerland.

At Fortunate Fields, Frank was introduced to a female German shepherd named Kiss. He could not abide the name and immediately changed it to "Buddy." The two went through extensive training until both dog and man felt comfortable with each other. Frank was delighted by the independence a guide dog could bring him. In one poignant moment, Frank told Eustis he wanted a haircut. She suggested Buddy lead him to the barber. All his life, Frank had been able to find someone to guide him to special events, but the mundane chores of life caused greater problems. It was easier to convince someone to take him to a concert than to a barber. But with Buddy's help, Frank realized he could go anywhere at any time.

Frank and Buddy completed their training and made a momentous journey back to the United States. On alighting from the ship, they were surrounded by a group of curious reporters. Frank eagerly described Buddy's intelligence and abilities at great length. Finally one skeptical reporter dared Frank to have Buddy lead him across West Street, through some of the most dangerous traffic in New York City. Buddy performed flawlessly, guiding Frank through the oncoming trucks, cars, and taxis until they were both safely on the other side. The newspaper reporters, impressed, wrote enthusiastic articles about the event.

All this good publicity was important. Morris Frank was not content with finding his own freedom; he was determined to benefit as many blind people as possible by promoting the use of guide dogs. He traveled around the country, demonstrating Buddy's ability to lead him safely across the busiest city streets in America. Eventually Frank helped Dorothy Eustis and Jack Humphrey found a school called "The Seeing Eye," where guide dogs and blind people were taught how to work with each other. With Buddy demonstrating how useful and well-behaved a guide dog could be, Frank lobbied to have guide dogs allowed in public places, including restaurants and airplanes.

In the course of their travels, Buddy was credited with saving Frank's life at least three times — once by pulling him out of the path of a team of runaway horses; once by blocking his way as he walked toward an empty elevator shaft; and once by waking him when the hotel where they were staying caught fire.

Even more important than her private devotion to Morris Frank was the fact that Buddy served as a living example of the value of Seeing Eye dogs. She demonstrated to an entire country that blind people need not be confined by their disability, that given a bit of freedom blind people could be productive members of society.

By 1994 guide dogs were helping more than 10,000 people in the United States, all of them owing a piece of their freedom to Morris Frank and his Seeing Eye dog, Buddy.

> *Today's aid dogs help people with all kinds of disabilities …*

WALLABY

Seeing Eye dogs are still the most well-known aid dogs, but others are being trained to help the hearing impaired and people with all manners of disabilities. One example is the story of Margo Gatheright-Dietrich, who suffered from a degenerative hip condition that eventually confined her to a wheelchair. An organization called Canine Companions for Independence matched up Gatheright-Dietrich with Wallaby, a yellow Labrador retriever. Wallaby could respond to more than sixty commands to perform tasks that are mundane for most people, but that were impossible for Gatheright-Dietrich to do for herself. From picking up dropped items to turning on a light switch, Wallaby took over where Gatheright-Dietrich's body failed her. When Gatheright-Dietrich was named Canine Companions' national ambassador in 1992, she said, "I could hire people to do all of the things that Wallaby does for me, but not only would it cost a great deal of money and rob me of my personal dignity, there's no one I could hire who would wake me up each and every morning with a big kiss and a wagging tail."

40

Bobbie *Scottish collie*

BOBBIE

A simple stone monument stands in the Humane Society cemetery in Portland, Oregon, next to a fancy wooden doghouse. Together they commemorate the journey of Bobbie of Silverton, who in 1923 performed one of the most singular acts of loyalty ever recorded.

Frank Brazier and his family bought Bobbie, a small Scottish collie mixed with a little shepherd, at the age of six weeks, and he came to live with them on their Oregon farm. As the little dog grew, he showed a natural aptitude for farm life and became something of a heeler, herding cats, livestock, and even humans in whatever direction he wanted them to go. Bobbie was also accident-prone. A horse kicked him, leaving a scar over his eye; a tractor ran over him (fortunately in soft earth, allowing him to escape with only a slight scar); and he broke two teeth trying to dig a gopher out of its hole. All these markings gave Bobbie a physical appearance as distinctive as his personality.

In 1923, a lost Scottish collie embarked on a remarkable journey across America to find his family.

After trying their hand at farming, the Brazier family decided to move into town and bought the Reo Cafe in Silverton, Oregon. Frank Brazier thought a dog used to running free on a farm would dislike the city, so he sold Bobbie to the friend who was buying their farm. Within a short time, however, Bobbie had left the farm and located the Braziers at their restaurant. For a while Bobbie visited the family on weekends and returned to the farm during the week.

About the same time the family decided to take a trip to Indiana, they bought Bobbie back. With the dog perched on the running board, the family drove their touring car east in August of 1923. The Braziers reached their destination of Wolcott, Indiana, and visited friends and relatives there. One day Frank Brazier took Bobbie in the car as he drove to a filling station. While he was inside the station, Brazier heard Bobbie's yelp. He raced out of the building just in time to see his little dog disappear around a corner with three or four town strays in hot pursuit.

Knowing Bobbie's ability to find the family, Brazier didn't worry at first. But Bobbie didn't return as expected. The family searched the town, driving around honking the car horn, expecting Bobbie to come running. When he didn't, the family started calling everyone they knew and even put an advertisement in the local paper. Still no Bobbie. The Braziers had to return home. Frank Brazier left instructions with his friends that if Bobbie were found he was to be shipped to Oregon. The family toured further in Indiana and Ohio, then turned west for home.

Time passed and the Braziers heard no word about their dog. The family returned to normal routines, sadder for the loss of their pet. Then, six months to the day since Bobbie disappeared, Frank Brazier's stepdaughter Nova was walking along a street in Silverton when she spotted a shaggy, bedraggled-looking dog. When she called out "Bobbie!" the dog ran to her. Nova could tell it was him because of the scars he'd received on the farm years before.

What followed was a happy reunion with the entire family as one after another greeted their long-lost pet. Somehow Bobbie had found his way across most of America — 2,551 miles by the Braziers' car odometer.

Actually, Bobbie had traveled farther than that. Word of his journey spread and eventually reached newspapers nationwide. As people across the country read of the little dog's travels, those who had seen him along the way began writing to the Braziers, describing their encounters with Bobbie.

From those letters, a member of the Oregon Historical Society pieced together some of the details of Bobbie's trip across the country. Apparently, after several days of prowling Wolcott, he headed northeast, going some 160 miles in the wrong direction. Later he was spotted on the outskirts of Indianapolis. Someone saw him swim the White River. He joined hoboes in their camps and probably traveled with them. He swam two more rivers and crossed Illinois. Somehow he crossed the Mississippi River; correspondents reported seeing him in Vinton, Iowa, then Des Moines. Still casting about, Bobbie went another 200 miles out of his way and returned to Des Moines.

Then something changed. Bobbie had been in Des Moines on Thanksgiving Day. Instead of wandering more false trails, he started on a straight course west. Six days later he reached Denver. With winter coming on, Bobbie left behind a family that wanted to adopt him and headed into the mountains. Six weeks later, having crossed the Rockies in December, Bobbie somehow found his way across the Snake River and trotted into Oregon along the Columbia River.

By the time he reached Portland, Bobbie's health was failing. It was there that Mary Elizabeth Smith took him into her home. Smith found Bobbie almost helpless: his legs were swollen, his feet were cut and gashed, and the pads on them were worn to the bone. Bobbie accepted her ministerings until he had regained some of his strength. She said later he had stood up stiffly, walked to the door, and indicated he wanted to go out. She watched as the dog limped down her path and turned south toward Silverton.

Two weeks later, Bobbie and Nova recognized each other on the streets of Silverton. By recreating the path of his trip, the Braziers calculated that Bobbie had traveled more than 3,000 miles in the search for his family.

While Bobbie rested and recuperated, the story of his amazing journey spread throughout the world. "Bobbie the Wonder Dog" was the subject of a popular children's book, a movie, and countless newspaper articles. The letters from people who had seen Bobbie on his journey were followed by thousands more from his admirers. Travelers detoured to Silverton to get a look at the dog who had crossed the country to find his family. Bobbie was presented with medals and the key to the city of Silverton. That spring, Bobbie was an honored guest at Portland's Home Beautiful Exposition, where he was given a luxurious "miniature bungalow" to live in, complete with windows and silk curtains, and where crowds gathered to see him.

While Bobbie recovered to a point, his journey had taken its toll. Doctors reported that by traveling through the winter and eating whatever he could chase down, Bobbie had caused permanent damage to his health. In March of 1927 Bobbie died in Silverton at the age of six.

Some dogs just refuse to give up on a scent ...

SAUR

While other tracking dogs have received more publicity, a Doberman pinscher named Saur holds the apparent record for the longest distance following a single scent. According to the *Guinness Book of World Records*, in 1925, while being handled by Herbert Kruger, Saur tracked a cattle thief more than one hundred miles across the Great Karoo in South Africa. 🐾

43

ENDURANCE · FIDELITY

INTELLIGENCE

44

Balto & Togo *Malemute, Siberian husky*

TOGO & BALTO

Wherever there are races, there are arguments. Teenagers argue Fords and Chevys. Horsemen argue thoroughbreds and quarter horses. In Nome, Alaska, arguments surrounded the All-Alaska Sweepstakes, a sled dog race in the early 1900s in which various companies owned the dog teams and hired the drivers. Owners of the popular malemute regularly argued with fans of the Siberian husky, recently imported from Siberia.

One proponent of the Siberian was Leonhard Seppala. A Norwegian by birth, Seppala arrived in Nome to prospect for gold in 1901. According to his biography, he quickly tired of that and, having learned to drive dogs, hired his services to the Hammon Consolidated Gold Fields Company.

During his time in Nome, Seppala trained and drove dogs for the mining company and entered many of the races sponsored by the Nome Kennel Club. His Siberians were consistent champions. But his greatest race was not against other dog teams, but against time and weather and a deadly epidemic of diphtheria that threatened the children of Nome in January of 1925.

Diphtheria was diagnosed in several children by Nome's Dr. Curtis Welch that month. Nome desperately needed the serum that would save the children, but airplanes couldn't fly through the rough weather to reach the Bering Sea city. So a doctor in Anchorage organized a sled dog relay to bring the medicine from the closest railroad stop, in Nenana, 650 miles across Alaska to Nome.

The city fathers sent Seppala to meet the medicine at the village of Nulato on the Yukon River, a distance of more than 300 miles. Seppala left Nome with twenty dogs, planning to leave a few in villages along the way to rest so he could pick them back up, refreshed, for the trip back. In front of the team was his favorite lead dog, a Siberian named Togo who Seppala had raised and trained himself.

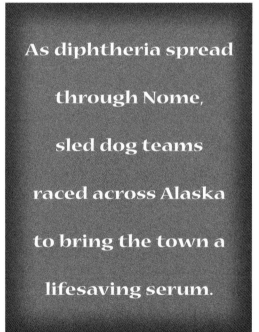

As diphtheria spread through Nome, sled dog teams raced across Alaska to bring the town a lifesaving serum.

With Togo in lead, Seppala pushed his way along the south coast of the Seward Peninsula toward Unalakleet, where there was a portage through the mountains to the Interior. At Isaac's Point, Seppala faced a choice. He could set out across the dangerous sea ice on Norton Sound, or he could take the safer but longer trail around the east end of the sound. He'd heard reports that the pack ice had been moving and was unstable, but he set out across the ice despite the hazard.

Trusting his dogs to lead him around any open water, Seppala almost reached the far shore of the sound when his dogs stopped. He watched them raise their ears and reach for scent with their noses, a clear indication that other dogs were nearby. Then he heard a call. He let the dogs move toward whatever it was they were smelling, and together they came upon another dog team.

It was driven by musher Henry Ivanoff, from the Eskimo village of Unalakleet. Ivanoff explained that he was the last in a chain of more than twenty mushers who had been recruited to relay the serum through the –50° and –60° F temperatures of the Interior and get it into Seppala's hands. If Seppala would take the serum back toward Nome, he would soon meet up with other mushers from Nome who would carry it the rest of the way.

Ivanoff handed the medicine over to Seppala, who immediately packed it into the sled and turned back toward Nome. This time he attempted an even shorter route, going straight northwest from Cape Denbeigh to Cape Darby. On this more treacherous

trail his dogs fell through thin ice, and Seppala spent several terror-filled moments bringing them back onto a solid surface. The team passed Cape Darby and raced for the village of Golovin.

There he gave the serum to Charlie Olson, who headed west toward Nome. About thirty miles down the trail, Olson reached the outpost at Bluff where Gunnar Kaasen was waiting. Like Seppala, Kaasen worked for the Hammon Company, and many of the dogs he drove had been trained by Seppala, including a malamute leader named Balto. With his fresh team and Balto in the lead, Kaasen raced toward Safety, an outpost just twenty-two miles east of Nome. There Kaasen was supposed to meet one last dog team that would take the serum to town.

Instead, Kaasen passed Safety and headed right for Nome. He later was quoted in the *New York Times* as saying that the dogs felt good and were making good time, so he thought he'd just go on. Another report claimed that Kaasen, fighting a blinding storm, missed Safety accidentally. For whatever reason, Kaasen pushed on into a growing blizzard. Along that part of the coast, storms often send winds howling through the valleys, blasting travelers with the driving snow. Kaasen, Balto, and the rest of the dogs battled that storm for hours, then triumphantly emerged from it on Nome's Front Street to deliver the serum.

The *New York Times*, receiving reports by telegraph first from Nome, then from Anchorage and Fairbanks, had followed the "race against death" every day for more than a week. When the crisis was finally over, it was only natural for the paper to make a hero out of the lead dog who had brought the serum to Nome. Balto became a hero worldwide, a symbol of strength and devotion and endurance, the dog who saved Nome.

Balto became a hero to everyone, except perhaps his owner and trainer. Leonhard Seppala maintained to his death that the true hero of the serum run was Togo, who had led Seppala's team almost 180 miles on very little rest, and who had saved the team time and time again on the moving ice of Norton Sound.

Who was the greater hero? Balto, with his statue in New York's Central Park, or Togo, the driver's own choice? Like most racing arguments, this one probably will never be resolved. Nor does it matter. Both dogs did their part according to their abilities. If Balto has become a symbol of that race against death, he stands for all the dogs who participated, all of the heroes who raced to save the children of Nome.

> *On September 18, 1957, a husky named Bravo walked around the world three times ...*

BRAVO

A husky mix who weighed 106 pounds on his first birthday, Bravo accompanied the first group of men to winter at the South Pole. Born in Antarctica, the dog seemed the natural companion for members of the International Geophysical Year project. On September 18, 1957, Bravo ventured out with Dr. Paul Siple and Jack Tuck to take a walk in –102° F temperatures. The three of them followed a row of red flags toward the circle where they'd marked the South Pole. Bravo ran ahead and reached the pole before the others. He circled the area at least three times before the other two arrived. They too made the circuit, traveling around 360 degrees of longitude in almost the same short time. After the winter, the men returned to the United States as heroes. Then the Navy tried to sell Bravo as surplus. Dr. Siple, who had gone to Antarctica with Admiral Byrd in 1929, fought to save the dog. Eventually Bravo was proclaimed a Very Important Dog, given an honorable discharge, and turned over to Tuck, who had raised him from a pup.

Hachi-ko *Akita*

秋田犬

HACHI-KO

Sometimes one dog's story can capture the admiration of an entire country. In this case, a faithful dog became a symbol for the Japanese people, the embodiment of one of their most treasured virtues — loyalty to family.

Born in Honshu Island's Akita Prefecture, from which the Akita breed draws its name, a young purebred Akita won the affection of a Mr. Kurita, a former agriculture student at Tokyo Imperial University. Like many agricultural students of the day, Kurita had been influenced greatly by a professor named Eizaburo Ueno. Recalling his former professor's affection for Akitas, Kurita bought the four-month-old pup and sent him to his teacher in January of 1924.

Affection between the professor and the dog was immediate. The professor named the pup "Hachi" and added "ko," a common term of endearment. For his part, Hachi-ko accompanied the professor everywhere he could. As he grew, Hachi-ko took on the traditional traits of an Akita: his ears stood upright,

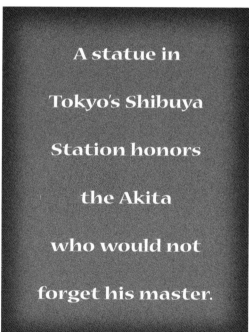

A statue in Tokyo's Shibuya Station honors the Akita who would not forget his master.

and his tail curled up and to the left. Professor Ueno reportedly took great pride in owning a purebred dog from a breed that had a history going back thirty centuries— especially as the number of purebred Akitas in Japan was dwindling at the time.

Professor Ueno lived in a well-to-do residential area of Tokyo. He enjoyed his morning walks to Shibuya Station, where he caught his train to the university every day. Hachi-ko joined the professor each morning, trotting along to the station, then returning home for the day. At 4 p.m. when the train arrived bringing the returning professor, Hachi-ko would be on the platform to welcome his master and walk home with him.

A year and a half into their routine, on a bright May day in 1925, Hachi-ko made his usual journey to the station to meet the professor at four o'clock. When the train stopped, it discharged its passengers, but Hachi-ko saw no sign of his beloved professor. That day Mr. Ueno had suffered a stroke and died in his laboratory at the university. He would never descend from the train again.

Hachi-ko searched the crowd for his master. Eventually the distraught dog went home. Each day he returned to the station to meet the morning and evening trains, but never found his master. Mrs. Ueno closed the house and moved, giving Hachi-ko to some of her husband's relatives who lived several miles from the station. The Akita refused to stay with them. As soon as he was let out, he trotted back first to his old house, then to the train station to await his master.

Professor Ueno's gardener, Kikuzaburo Kobayashi, lived close to the station and took over Hachi-ko's care. From the gardener's home, the dog began a regular routine of walking to the train station in the morning and then to his master's former home for the day. At four o'clock he was waiting on the platform to meet the afternoon train. As time passed, Hachi-ko stopped going to his master's home but continued to go to the station every time he was untied.

In the first years of his vigil, Hachi-ko was treated as little more than a tolerable nuisance at the train station. In 1928, a new stationmaster came to Shibuya Station. He quickly grew very fond of Hachi-ko and allowed him free run of the facility. Hachi-ko still kept his schedule, but also was allowed to remain in the station through the day, sleeping in a storeroom set aside for him by the new stationmaster.

That same year, another of Professor Ueno's former students, who had become something of an expert on Akitas, saw the dog at the station and followed him to the Kobayashi home, where he learned the history of Hachi-ko's life. Shortly after this meeting, the former student published a documented census of Akitas in Japan. His research found only thirty purebred Akitas remaining, including the dog at Shibuya station.

Professor Ueno's former student returned frequently to visit the dog and over the years published several articles about Hachi-ko's remarkable loyalty. In 1932 one of these articles, published in Tokyo's largest newspaper, threw the dog into the national spotlight. Hachi-ko became a sensation throughout the land. His faithfulness to his master's memory impressed the people of Japan as a spirit of family loyalty all should strive to achieve. Teachers and parents used Hachi-ko's vigil as an example for children to follow. A well-known Japanese artist rendered a sculpture of the dog, and throughout the country a new awareness of the Akita breed grew.

In 1934, through the efforts of the former student, the stationmaster, and the artist, a statue of Hachi-ko was commissioned. Efforts began to raise money for the statue, and the majority of contributions came from schoolchildren. Dignitaries unveiled the statue in front of the station in April of 1934 in a grand ceremony that included bouquets of flowers, speeches, and Hachi-ko himself looking on.

For all his fame, the dog continued his watch at

the station. Growing older, he seldom ventured from the building, only occasionally walking to the Kobayashi home for a meal. One day in March of 1935, people at the station missed seeing Hachi-ko at his usual hangouts. A quickly organized search found him lying prone in a lane nearby. None of the veterinarians from the university who had cared for him over the years could save the dog. He was taken back to his own bed in the station, where he died later in the day. His skin and skeleton were preserved, and friends buried Hachi-ko's other remains near his master's grave.

Hachi-ko's influence did not end with his death. In 1937 famed American lecturer Helen Keller visited his statue at Shibuya Station. She was so affected by Hachi-ko's story that when she later visited Akita City, she asked for an Akita dog. One presented to her at the time died shortly thereafter, but a second was sent to her home and is believed to have been the first Akita in the United States.

The legend of Hachi-ko's nine-year vigil goes on. The bronze statue of Hachi-ko was melted down for metal during World War II, but after the war a new statue was made and placed on its pedestal outside the station. Today the statue remains an important symbol to the Japanese. It has become a tradition for friends and lovers to meet there, possibly hoping that some of Hachi-ko's undying loyalty will rub off on them.

FANG

Some dogs never forget a good deed, or forgive a bad one ...

In the mid-1600s, an English squire named Alexander Iden was walking through his estate along the Thames River when he spotted an Irish wolfhound swimming to a small mudflat island. Over time, Iden saw the dog swim to the island as many as three times a day. He began feeding the dog and befriended it. One day, Iden followed the dog to the island and there he found a mound of dirt. Under the mound, Iden found the remains of a man who obviously had been murdered. He ordered the body taken back to the mainland for a proper burial. From then on, the dog, who Iden had named Fang, visited the new grave as often as he'd visited the island before. Sometime later, Iden made a trip to London for supplies. He was negotiating with some boatmen to transport the goods to his estate when suddenly Fang launched himself at one of the boatmen, attacking viciously. Confronted by the angry dog, the boatman confessed to killing the dog's owner and burying him on the island. A few days later, after Fang again snarled at the man in the magistrate's court, the murderer was hanged in a public London square.

Buster *Spitz*

BUSTER

As Mr. and Mrs. Frank Remackel slept in their Minneapolis apartment on the night of April 13, 1931, they had no idea what one of their neighbors was doing in a nearby room. Somewhere in that apartment building a man had punched a hole in his wall and stuffed it with tissue. For whatever reason, the Remackels' neighbor touched a match to the paper and ignited a fire that soon spread through the entire building.

Asleep in the Remackels' apartment, their black and tan spitz, Buster, snuggled next to his playmate, a Persian cat named Fluffy. The two animals had been close friends for most of their lives. Shortly before the fire, Buster had saved Fluffy from a small trap. The dog had found the cat snared in the trap, unable to move or escape. Lifting Fluffy gently by the nape of the neck, Buster carried his friend and the trap to Mrs. Remackel, who carefully released the cat.

Now the two animals were inseparable and even slept together, as they were on the night when hints of smoke began wafting into their home. Buster, smelling the smoke, rose from his sleeping rug in the kitchen and trotted to Mrs. Remackel's bedroom. He put his nose to her pillow and began licking her face. A bothersome dog saying good morning at 4 a.m. isn't the most welcome intrusion. Mrs. Remackel pushed Buster away at first. But Buster wouldn't stop. He jumped up on the bed and tried to pull off the covers, barking loudly. When this still didn't rouse his mistress, Buster clamped his jaws around her arm, hard enough to give her a start but not quite hard enough to break the skin. That brought her to life.

Waking to the smell of smoke in the apartment, Mrs. Remackel struggled to her feet and into a robe, then shuffled off to find her husband, who had fallen asleep in another room. When both were standing, Buster ran to the front door and threw his whole body against it. Beginning to feel the effects of the smoke, the Remackels followed

> In 1931, a pet dog saved thirty-five people — plus one special friend — from a disastrous fire.

their dog to the door.

Once the door was open, Buster ran into the hallway, but he wasn't satisfied with having saved his own family. The little spitz ran to the next apartment. Yapping wildly, he began throwing himself against that door. He scratched and scratched at the door until he heard a commotion inside. Assured that the residents were awake, Buster ran to the next apartment and started scratching at that door. By this time smoke had begun filling the hallways. One after another, doors opened and people began finding their way out of the building. As the building's residents stumbled through the smoke, Buster continued his noisy alarm at the doors of other apartments.

At one door, he received no response. Buster threw himself against the door again and again, but still no one answered from inside. According to reports from the incident, Buster weakened the door hardware so much that the latch gave way and allowed him into the apartment. He raced through the place until he found an elderly man asleep in a bedroom. As he had with his mistress, Buster jumped onto the bed, barking, growling, and pulling at the covers.

When the man finally sat up, he smelled the smoke and made an effort to rise. An amputee, the resident had to find the prosthesis for his missing leg. Buster ran around the bed barking, attempting to hurry the man's efforts. Once the artificial leg was in place, the man found his robe and his cane, and followed Buster to the door. By this time, heat from

the fire had grown intense and both struggled against the thickening smoke as they made their way through the halls toward the door. Buster stayed with his charge until both reached the front door of the building and began descending the steps to the sidewalk.

Outside, Buster heard Mrs. Remackel calling and ran to her. But something was wrong. Buster sniffed around his mistress, raced through the crowd gathering in the street, then went back to Mrs. Remackel again. She said later that Buster gave her a pleading look, then turned and raced back into building. In their haste to escape, the Remackels had forgotten Buster's pal, the cat, Fluffy.

What happened then only could be surmised. As the story was pieced together later, Buster was slowed by the dense smoke, but still found his way to his own apartment. Inside, the smoke had turned to flame; against a wall of heat, Buster yelped for his buddy. Fluffy emerged from hiding, shaking and afraid. Like a sheepdog, Buster herded the cat toward the door and out into the corridor. Nipping at heels, barking, nudging, he drove Fluffy toward the street. The two animals emerged from the smoke into the welcoming arms of their owners.

The fire burned out of control, eventually gutting the building. Fire inspectors later would discover the cause of the blaze and arrest the man responsible.

Out on the street, thirty-five people watched the fire, probably lamenting their loss, but thankful that the determination of one dog had saved them all. No one suffered even a minor injury.

The story of Buster's bravery was published in several Minneapolis newspapers and attracted the attention of the Latham Foundation, a humane organization headquartered in California that promotes respect for animals through education. In 1932, Buster was presented with the Latham Foundation's highest honor, its Gold Medal award.

BILL

The Moore family was used to the ore trains that roared through the mining district around Holden, Washington, in 1926. Though their yard was unfenced, their two-year-old son Richard played there, and Mrs. Moore assumed he knew to be leery of the trains that passed their yard. One day she was out hanging clothes with Richard nearby. An approaching train didn't raise any apprehensions; her son was used to them. She worked with her back to both. Then she glanced

Suddenly, when it's least expected, the family dog becomes a true hero ...

around the yard. Unable to spot her son, she turned to the tracks, where she saw Richard wandering between the rails. The roar of the approaching train drowned her shouts as she ran toward the tracks. The engineer, seeing the child on the tracks, laid on his whistle, but that only frightened the boy and paralyzed him. Suddenly there was a flash of brown and white. The family's English pointer, Bill, streaked toward the child on the tracks. Just as the train was about to reach the boy, Bill slammed into Richard and knocked him off the tracks into a ditch. Mrs. Moore, unable to see what had happened, screamed frantically until the train had passed. When the last car rumbled by, she crossed the tracks to find the boy on his back in the ditch. Bill was standing with his forepaws on Richard's chest, unwilling to let the boy rise until the danger had passed. For his courage and quick action, Bill was nominated for the Latham Foundation's Gold Medal award.

56

Chips *German shepherd/collie/husky*

CHIPS

As a pet in Pleasantville, New York, Chips did much to endear himself to his family. What the rest of the town thought was another matter. A combination of German shepherd, collie, and husky, Chips had the head of a shepherd and the body of a husky with its signature bushy tail. Chips appointed himself the family's official guardian. He followed young Gail Wren to school and spent the day lying by her desk — to the chagrin of the teacher, who was afraid to chase the dog away. He escorted Mrs. Wren to the dentist, ensuring a gentle job by the doctor. Chips also defended the Wren home from various intruders, like postmen and delivery boys.

Just after the outbreak of World War II, on a day when the dog had saved his home from an invading garbage man, Edward Wren decided Chips had definite military inclinations. So Wren donated the dog to Dogs for Defense, a civilian organization supplying recruits for the army's new K-9 Corps.

Chips's attack on an enemy machine-gun nest made him one of the most famous dogs of World War II.

The army sent Chips to its War Dog Training Center in Fort Royal, Virginia. After his training in 1942, Chips was shipped out with the Thirtieth Infantry, Third Infantry Division, prior to the invasion of North Africa. He was one of the first four such dogs sent overseas. Under fire from the shore and the air, Chips rode in an amphibious tank onto a beach in French Morocco and dug in with the rest of the troops. As the Allied forces fought their way across the African continent, Chips served mostly as a sentry, guarding camps from the enemy and from thieving locals.

During the campaign, Chips stood guard at the house where American President Franklin Roosevelt met with British Prime Minister Winston Churchill in Casablanca in January 1943. After their conference, the two great leaders reviewed the troops and, reports indicate, met the dog who had protected them.

The discussion between Churchill and Roosevelt

was to have a great impact on Chips's life. As the campaign in Africa raced to its conclusion, the Allies already had formed the plan for a final victory in Europe. Part of that plan involved the invasion of Sicily and Italy, and a pinscher movement into northern Europe. Chips and his unit joined the vanguard of the push.

At the beginning, the Seventh Army under General George Patton massed an amphibious assault off the coast of Sicily. In the pre-dawn darkness of July 10, 1943, Chips huddled with his handler, Private John Rowell, aboard an army landing craft awaiting the word to go. The landing craft moved toward shore, thumped on the beach, dropped its ramp, and released the troops and the dog into murderous fire from shoreside Italian gun positions.

As Allied troops attempted to gain a foothold on the beach, fire came from almost every direction. Artillery shells exploded on the beach. Machine-gun fire raked the invading soldiers. Flares overhead lit up the targets for the bunkered Italian gunners. Through all of this, the Americans crawled from foxhole to foxhole up the beach.

Chips and Rowell and the rest of their unit gained a small handhold on the beach, but directly in front of them was an Italian bunker, its heavy gunfire pinning them into the sand. The bunker commanded a wide portion of the beach, immobilizing most of the invading unit. Unable to move, unable to shout for help over the noise, Rowell wondered if he'd live through the invasion.

Then Chips growled and rose. Outrunning Rowell's protests, Chips charged up the beach toward the bunker. The Italian gunners aimed at the running dog, their bullets kicking up sprays of sand in his path. One bullet nipped Chips's scalp. Another tore into his hip, staggering him for a second, but Chips ran on toward the bunker.

Rowell watched Chips charge over a barricade and disappear into the bunker. The gun went silent. For seconds, Rowell could only guess what was happening inside the gun placement. Then an Italian soldier emerged from the bunker, screaming. Chips held a death grip on the soldier's neck as the man clawed at him, trying to escape the furor of the canine attack. Behind the first man, three others marched out of the bunker indicating their willingness to surrender.

Rowell's unit quickly took the Italians prisoner, gaining the bunker and some measure of safety. Rowell tended the dog's wounds as he could, and later Chips went to the rear for more serious treatment. Besides the scalp and hip wounds, Chips had burned his mouth, apparently by grabbing the hot barrel of the machine gun.

When he had recovered, Chips rejoined Rowell and his unit and fought with them through Italy, France, Germany, and Austria until the end of the war. For his attack against the machine-gun bunker, Chips's commanding officer nominated the dog for the Silver Star for bravery and the Purple Heart for his wounds. During a ceremony at Pietravairano, Italy, Division General Lucian Truscott Jr. pinned the Silver Star to the dog's collar, saying "Chips's courageous act, single-handedly eliminating a dangerous machine-gun nest, reflects the highest credit on himself and the military service."

Later, the War Department thought better of giving one of its highest awards to a dog and revoked the medals. That probably didn't bother Chips's canine mind, but in an ironic way he still exacted his revenge for the lost medals.

Later in the war, when Supreme Allied Commander Dwight Eisenhower visited the Third Division, he was introduced to Chips. The dog, however, had been trained to be wary of strangers making uneven moves around him. So when Eisenhower bent to pet Chips, the dog promptly bit the general's hand.

The army discharged Chips in 1945 and returned him to his family. With him he took an unofficial medal awarded by his own unit, a theater ribbon with a star for each of the eight campaigns in which he'd fought.

Weakened by the travails of war, Chips died at the Wren family home in 1947. He was buried in an unmarked grave at the Hartsdale Canine Cemetery in Westchester County, New York.

Never underestimate the power of a canine warrior ...

PERITES

Alexander the Great received a dog named Perites as a gift from a lesser monarch seeking his favor. Told the dog was a great hunter, Alexander tried him out in the battle ring, but Perites showed no interest in fighting several small animals. Alexander thought of returning the gift, but decided to try Perites on something more challenging. Into the battle ring soldiers released a lion, who attacked immediately. According to legend, Perites killed the lion in less than a minute. Then Alexander ordered an elephant to be released into the ring. Nimbly avoiding tusks and feet, Perites fought the elephant until, exhausted and confused, it lay down in the dirt. From that moment on, Alexander and his pet were inseparable. One night, as Alexander's armies were resting from their marches across Asia, an assassin slipped past the guards. He crept into the tent where Alexander lay sleeping. Just as the assassin raised his knife, Perites awoke and attacked, driving the assailant to the ground. One pinprick from the poisoned dagger left Perites dying. Later Alexander named one of the cities he conquered "Perite" in his dog's honor.

60

Beauty *Wire-haired terrier*

BEAUTY

For those who did not live through it, the horror of the London Blitz can only be imagined. It was one of the largest assaults on a civilian population in wartime history. Night after night, sirens wailed and people ran for shelters. The unmistakable sound of German bombers droned overhead; then the bombs fell. In the movies they sometimes whistle; in reality they dropped silently, smashing homes and businesses, trapping families under tons of rubble. Those bombers that survived their encounters with British fighter planes turned back toward Germany. When the all-clear sounded, survivors emerged from their hiding places to survey the damage. Rescue squads also appeared — people who volunteered to search the debris for anyone trapped in the wreckage of the bombed-out buildings.

One of those volunteers was a man named Bill Barnett who operated a mobile clinic for the People's Dispensary for Sick Animals, a veterinary charity.

> During the London Blitz, this wire-haired terrier helped rescue sixty-three animals trapped in the rubble.

The PDSA offered care for sick and injured animals belonging to owners too poor to afford normal veterinary service. Shortly before the war, somebody delivered a litter of wire-haired terriers to the clinic. Among the pups, Barnett found one who immediately endeared herself to him. Once the puppy was strong enough to move, Barnett took her home. His wife, when she saw the puppy, said, "Oh, what a beauty!" inspiring the dog's name.

Early in her life, Beauty displayed a remarkable hearing ability. She recognized the sound of her master's automobile from a block away. She could distinguish footfalls among the family's acquaintances. Beauty also learned a tolerance for other animals by accompanying Barnett to his clinic and sitting quietly as he treated the pets of London's poor.

When World War II began and brought with it the bombers over London, Barnett's work took on a new dimension. As searchers sought human survi-

Dog Heroes

vors of the bombing, the PDSA was called upon to rescue their pets. The PDSA's work saved injured and dying animals; it restored them to their worried owners; and it prevented London from being overrun by homeless, starving, perhaps feral animals.

On one venture into the rubble of a destroyed building early in the war, Barnett and his crew were searching for survivors. One of the workers noticed that Beauty wasn't following them as usual, but instead was staring intently at a particular spot in the debris. She started scratching at the surface. Barnett decided to follow his dog's example, and he suggested the other workers also dig in that area. Fifteen feet down, cowering under a kitchen table, was the homeowner's cat, still lively enough to spit at its rescuer. Beauty had made her first rescue.

From then on, the rescuers watched Beauty as she moved through the rubble left by the bombs and followed her lead to rescue the pets of London. In the course of her career, the little dog received credit for finding sixty-three animals, probably by hearing their movement under the wreckage. The first dog used for such a task, Beauty inspired the employment of others. Soon dogs throughout England were searching for survivors of the Blitz.

Beauty worked through the entire war. As she helped dig out victims, she often injured her own paws, breaking and shattering nails, and rubbing her pads raw in the rocky rubble. Unable to dissuade her from digging, Barnett had boots fashioned from chamois leather to protect her feet.

Some of Beauty's rescues were truly remarkable. During one search, Beauty gave the signal that her human companions recognized as indicating the location of a trapped animal. Although she normally joined in the digging, this time she walked away, apparently disinterested. Barnett wondered if Beauty could be sick or perhaps had made a mistake. Despite Beauty's odd behavior, the rescuers kept digging at the spot she had indicated. A short way down, they found a goldfish bowl that somehow had survived the bombing. Though a layer of dust floated on the surface of the water, a live goldfish was swimming around in the bowl.

In one of her most notable rescues, Beauty saved not only a pet but the rescue crew as well. The search party, including Beauty, entered a building that the bombs had left barely standing. After a quick search, the crew found the owner's dog quivering under a stairway. Rather than giving her usual response to a rescued animal, Beauty appeared agitated, trotting back and forth, yipping. The rescue party noticed her excitement. Probably nervous anyway in the unstable building, they grabbed the rescued dog and followed Beauty's lead to the door. Just as the last of the party cleared the threshold, there was a sound of stone grinding against stone, and then the building collapsed into a dust cloud. Beauty's warning had saved the whole crew.

As the war went on, Beauty became something of a celebrity. She joined the effort to raise money for the war, participating in parades entreating citizens to purchase war bonds. Because she had been the example that encouraged the use of dogs in rescue work, in 1941 the PSDA presented her with its Pioneer Medal, an honor usually reserved for humans. Early in 1945 she received Britain's highest award given to animals, the Dickin Medal for gallantry, an honor likened to the Victoria Cross for humans. She even was presented to Queen Elizabeth.

For Beauty herself, probably the greatest reward for her rescue work was a citation giving her the freedom to roam in one tightly restricted London park. The special proclamation gave her "the freedom of Holland Park and all the trees therein."

JUDY

When World War II broke out in the Far East, Judy already was a fixture on the Shanghai docks. A purebred English pointer, she attracted the attention of a British gunboat crew and joined them on their patrols of the Yangtze River. Her timely alarms often warned the crew of imminent attacks. When the boat went south for the Malay-Singapore campaign, Judy went along. Enemy fire sank the boat between Java and Singapore, and the men and dog took refuge on an uninhabited island. The men quickly discovered why the island had no residents; there seemed to be no fresh water. Judy saved them by discovering a small freshwater spring. The men eventually commandeered a fishing boat, but soon the Japanese intercepted their escape vessel and they were sent, along with Judy, to a prison camp. Fighting starvation every day for two years, the men had to steal what they ate. Judy served as the lookout on their forays and sounded the alarm when enemy guards approached. When the Japanese shipped the prisoners to Singapore, one of the men smuggled Judy aboard the ship. Then the prison ship was torpedoed, sending the men into the water. Judy swam with them until their rescue. The Japanese sailors who picked up the survivors, however, sent them to Sumatra, where they were used as slave labor to lay miles of railroad tracks.

In times of war, dogs often serve as faithful friends to those in need ...

After the war, Judy went to live with one of her friends in England. At the time Judy was recognized as the only dog ever officially registered as a prisoner of war.

63

Lassie *Collie*

LASSIE

The short story "Lassie Come Home" first appeared in the December 17, 1938, issue of the *Saturday Evening Post*. It told of a Scottish boy separated from his faithful collie and of the dog's thousand-mile journey across the rough Scottish landscape to rejoin his master. Readers responded so strongly to the story that author Eric Knight expanded it into a novel, which was published in 1940. By 1943, the story reached Hollywood, where a lack of scripts and, for that matter, movie stars prompted the Metro Goldwyn Mayer studio to begin production of a motion picture version.

To make the movie *Lassie Come Home*, the studio needed a star — not just a companion for a human actor, but a dog who could carry the lead role. Movie-makers had avoided collies in the past, finding them too temperamental for the long hours around the bustling movie sets. This role demanded a collie, though, so director Fred Wilcox began his search for the perfect Lassie.

Hollywood's greatest dog movie star began life as an unwanted, misbehaving collie puppy.

At his brand-new kennel in North Hollywood, trainer Rudd Weatherwax read an advertisement calling for a movie collie. He thought he had just the dog. In business for just a few weeks, Weatherwax had been hired to work with a collie named Pal, to train away some of his many bad habits. The dog chased motorcycles, barked constantly, chewed everything he could get his teeth around, and wasn't even housebroken. Though he was a full-blooded collie, Pal didn't meet show criteria. His eyes were too large, his head too broad, and his hair too dark for the minions of the dog show circuit. Weatherwax quickly recognized that, despite his drawbacks, Pal possessed tremendous intelligence. As the owner was happy to be rid of the poorly behaved collie, Weatherwax bought Pal for ten dollars and took him through six months of intensive training.

When the call came for a Lassie, Pal had been sent to a friend's ranch, where he had the freedom to roam until there was room for him again at the North

Dog Heroes

Hollywood kennel. Weatherwax came to retrieve Pal and take him to the tryout. But when Weatherwax called for Pal, the dog that came running didn't have the fine coat with the full ruff that Weatherwax had remembered. Instead, the dog's coat was a mess, all full of burrs, with patches of fur ripped out. Pal looked more like a pound dog than a movie star.

Weatherwax did what he could with Pal's coat and took the mangy-looking dog to the designated field for the tryout, where 300 other collies were also waiting. The movie producers didn't even give Pal a first glance. They walked right by without a nod. Still, they didn't find their perfect dog, either. When that tryout failed, Wilcox began a nationwide search. He settled on a beautiful show collie sometime later, but found that dog to be dumb and skittish. When the cameras started whirring, the show dog ran away and hid from the noise.

Weatherwax learned the movie crew still was looking for the perfect collie. By that time, Pal's coat had grown full again under his trainer's constant brushing and trimming. Weatherwax telephoned Wilcox to say he had "another dog" that would be perfect for the part. He was invited to a meeting and at this one, the carefully groomed Pal trotted up to Wilcox, sat on his haunches, and lifted his right paw to shake hands. Impressed, the director asked Weatherwax to put Pal through his paces. Once Pal had performed a series of exercises, mostly to silent hand commands, Wilcox called for a screen test. The physical deficiencies that had denied Pal show status proved to be attributes for a film star. His dark hair photographed well, and his large head projected the intelligence expected of Lassie's character. It was his eyes, though, those eyes too large for show judges, that emoted on the screen and gave him a personality that reached out to the audience. One day after his screen test, the studio signed Pal to a contract.

Pal's biggest test was yet to come. For the first scene filmed for *Lassie Come Home*, Pal had to swim the San Joaquin River, simulating Lassie's crossing of the Tweed River between Scotland and England. Weatherwax rowed Pal to the center of the river. At the indication from the director and a command from his trainer, Pal jumped from the boat into the river. He swam past another boat, containing a film crew, and headed right to a camera on shore. According to Weatherwax, Pal responded perfectly to his hand signals. When he reached shore, Pal climbed from the water, his tail between his legs and his head down, as if he were exhausted. He slinked to a point in front of the camera, laid down, and closed his eyes. The performance made even his trainer choke up. Wilcox commented to Weatherwax, "Pal jumped into that water, and Lassie climbed out."

Lassie Come Home opened to almost universally rave reviews. The *New York Times* reported that the movie provided "at least a partial solution to the present dearth of Hollywood leading men."

As Lassie, Pal made five more movies, starring with some of Hollywood's biggest stars, including Elizabeth Taylor. His sixth movie, *Challenge to Lassie*, written especially for Pal by Marjorie Kinnan Rawling, was based on the story of Greyfriars Bobby, which appears elsewhere in this book.

Lassie also had a radio show in which Pal barked, whined, and yelped on command to complement the voices of the human characters. In 1953 Lassie went to television in what would become one of the longest-running adventure shows ever. At least two generations of American children grew up with Lassie's pals — first Jeff, then Timmy — and watched her later adventures with the U.S. Forest Service. The show, starring seven generations of Lassies, ran for eighteen years and still appears in syndicated reruns.

Pal, the original Lassie, died at the age of nineteen, probably the richest and surely the most successful of all dog movie stars.

RIN TIN TIN

Some stories say Rin Tin Tin was found as a puppy in an abandoned German trench during World War I. Others claim a female German shepherd, an aviator's mascot, was rescued from a downed American airplane and shortly afterward gave birth to the famous pup. The American flier who adopted the puppy, Lee Duncan, named the dog after a charm doll French soldiers carried for luck. At home after the war, Duncan bought a ranch near Santa Monica, California, where "Rinty" learned to herd sheep, along with some

Many of the most famous canine celebrities have come from the humblest beginnings ...

more usual obedience tricks. The dog's talent for jumping fences and hedges caught the eye of a traveling newsreel photographer, and the subsequent film attracted the attention of the Warner Brothers studio. Signed to a contract quickly, Rin Tin Tin went on to make more than forty movies and become a hero to generations of children worldwide. Besides the action stunts he performed, Rinty was known for being one of the few dogs who could express emotion on screen, even changing his facial expressions at the direction of his trainer. Sons and grandsons carried on Rin Tin Tin's name and work through movies and television programs even into the 1990s. 🐾

67

68

Laika *Mongrel*

LAIKA

Some dogs, like certain Saint Bernards and German shepherds, are trained for acts of heroism or just take to them naturally. But other dogs are made heroes by circumstance, unwittingly placed in roles that allow them to help change human history forever. Such was the heroism, or perhaps simply the fate, of a Russian dog named Laika.

In the 1950s, the United States was in a period of prosperity. The Great Depression was over, as was World War II. Life seemed almost euphoric. People moved into new houses in suburbia. They watched as each year television brought new entertainments into their homes. Popular music grew to a crescendo, peaking with the Elvis Presley phenomenon. Each year, the introduction of new automobile models sent adults through showrooms and teenagers dreaming. Those new cars also symbolized the strength of American industry, the greatest in the world. Only one fear dampened the euphoria: the threat of the communist Soviet Union. Still, it was a cold war, Russia was far away, and — with the exception of the occasional

On November 3, 1957, Laika became the first living creature to orbit the earth.

family building a bomb shelter in its backyard — most people ignored the Russian threat in their search for a place in America's prosperity.

Then the Soviets changed all that with a 183-pound sphere called Sputnik. On October 4, 1957, the Soviet Union launched this satellite into space, where it circled the earth for a period of weeks. Americans were shaken. The Russians had beaten the United States into space, beaten American industry, beaten American ingenuity. Every few hours, Sputnik orbited the earth, passing right over American homes. Standing in their backyards, Americans strained to see the intruder cross the night sky.

Sputnik changed a generation. Suddenly the country was in the Space Race — and way behind. Students were pressured into majors that supported technology, and pressured away from anything that wouldn't help "catch the Russians." Scientists dropped other projects to support the American space effort. But before America was to have any success, Russia pushed ahead.

Dog Heroes

Even before the shock of Sputnik had abated, the Soviet government shot another rocket into space, this one releasing the 1,120-pound Sputnik II into orbit. On board was a passenger, the first living being to orbit the earth.

For this momentous event, the Soviets had chosen a dog to represent man in the great adventure. Laika, described either as a Samoyed, a Samoyed-husky mix, or a mongrel, weighed about eleven pounds. She was small, intelligent, tough, female, and obedient, all traits the Russians sought for their cosmic travelers. And she was almost pure white; reports from the time indicate the Russians preferred white dogs because they showed up better on pictures sent back from space.

After some time in training, Laika was prepared for her launch. Russian scientists cleaned her with an alcohol solution and combed every contaminant out of her coat. They covered her with iodine and put antiseptic powder on places where they would attach electrodes to monitor her various bodily functions.

Then the team placed her in the capsule, a cone-shaped satellite similar to Sputnik I but with an extra compartment for the dog. Laika was confined to the compartment with a harness. Her electrodes were attached, all systems checked and rechecked. On November 3, 1957, less than a month after Sputnik I, the rockets fired and carried the first dog into orbit.

As Sputnik II was launched into space, monitors sent back signals indicating that Laika was breathing normally and her pulse rate was normal.

Scientists also kept track of her skin and internal temperature, along with the cabin's air pressure and temperature. They noted that, at first, Laika resisted the effects of the launch but as she reached the highest rate of acceleration, she was pressed to the floor of her compartment. Her heartbeat increased to nearly three times its normal rate. By the time Sputnik II reached orbit, Laika's respiration was three to four times the normal rate.

Once in orbit, when she reached a state of weightlessness, Laika was able to rise and stand for short periods. Her pulse and respiration decreased almost to normal and she settled into a normal routine. Photos broadcast back from Sputnik II showed Laika was moving about and eating with little trouble as she reached a maximum height of 1,037 miles above the earth.

For six days Laika circled the earth. All the data gathered from her flight indicated that human beings could also survive in space. Despite the fears generated by Sputnik I, everyone had to cheer for the little dog in space and the momentous journey she was making for the good of mankind.

One problem that Soviet scientists could not solve at the time was how to return Laika safely to earth. After six days in orbit, Laika died in her capsule. The reason given was that the ship ran out of oxygen, as planned, or possibly that Laika had overheated from cosmic radiation.

Whatever the reason for her death, Laika had served as the first living being in orbit. Sputnik II circled the earth for five more months after Laika died, then plunged to earth, burning in the atmosphere as it fell. The satellite with the dog on board had completed 2,370 orbits and covered 62,500 miles, paving the way for more animals and eventually humans to follow Laika into space.

Not all Russian space dogs shared Laika's sad fate. In August of 1960, the Soviet Union sent two more dogs, named Belka and Strelka, into orbit. Both dogs were safely returned to earth, and Strelka later gave birth to a litter of healthy puppies. Soviet Premier Nikita Khrushchev gave one of the pups, named Pushinka, to the family of President John F. Kennedy, as a gift of goodwill between the two rival nations.

> *Some dogs are born to greatness, others have greatness thrust upon them ...*

MARJORIE

Marjorie was another dog who played an important role in the progress of human science. The black and white mongrel was used in an experiment at the University of Toronto. Dr. Frederick G. Banting and graduate student Charles H. Best had been searching for the hormone within the pancreas that regulates blood sugar. They discovered a strong, close-to-pure extract in unborn calves and named the hormone "insulin." Banting and Best made Marjorie diabetic by removing her pancreas so her blood sugar level dropped immediately. The two scientists first injected Marjorie with insulin on July 27, 1921. Using regular doses, they prolonged her life by seventy days, making her the first diabetic creature to be kept alive with insulin. Based on their experiments, Leonard Thompson, a thirteen-year-old diabetic, was given insulin the next January, becoming the first human patient to receive the therapy and leading the way for millions more diabetics the world over to live normal lives.

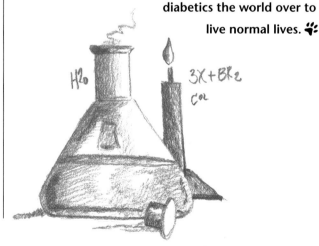

NOME

DITAROD TRAIL
* ALASKA *

™

THE LAST
GREAT RACE
™

ANCHORAGE

72

Andy *Alaska sled dog*

ANDY

Alaska Native villagers have a phrase they use to describe the perfect sled dog team leader. What they say is: "You could write your name in the snow." What they mean is the dog takes steering commands so well that a driver could call for the twists and turns of a script signature and the dog would lead the team precisely enough to write the name in fresh snow.

That phrase was used to describe Andy, a leader who four times won the Iditarod Trail Sled Dog Race, the 1,100-mile-long race from Anchorage to Nome held every March to commemorate the 1925 diphtheria serum run.

Andy, an Alaska sled dog, led his team to four victories in the 1,100-mile Iditarod.

Kennel club pedigrees don't mean much in the world of the Iditarod, but any successful musher can trace the lineage of his dogs several generations back. So while it's true that Andy's breed can be described only as "Alaska sled dog," it's more important that Andy's mother, Nugget, came from a line that produced many of the top dogs in the early years of the Iditarod.

Andy was born in the summer of 1975, in the second litter of pups raised by driver Rick Swenson in Eureka, Alaska. Swenson ran his first Iditarod the next spring, finishing tenth, which was to be his lowest place in the standings over the next seventeen years. Already Swenson had seen potential in Andy, but that first year the pup was just too young to go along. The next year, before he reached the age of two, Andy had proved himself as a leader. When Swenson left the starting line in Anchorage, Andy raced in lead. Along with him in the team were his mother and five siblings. Sixteen days and a few hours later, after crossing some 1,100 miles of Alaska wilderness trail, Andy led the team across the finish line in Nome, just five minutes ahead of the competition. It was Swenson's and Andy's first win, and the beginning of a string of top finishes that was to last well into the 1980s.

The end of the 1978 Iditarod found them racing down Front Street in Nome, collar-to-collar with a team driven by Iditarod veteran Dick Mackey. Mackey, slightly behind, pulled a whip from his sled, and the sound of one crack gave his team a surge of speed that pushed the leaders past Andy to win the race by a nose. The official time difference was one second, the closest finish ever.

By 1979, Swenson knew he'd found a lead dog to complement his own intense competitiveness. "Probably his most famous quality was he didn't want anyone in front of him," Swenson said.

One of the times when this quality really stood out was in the 1979 Iditarod. Emmitt Peters and Rick Swenson had been racing since McGrath, which is about a third of the way into the race. By that time, the racers have sorted themselves out according to their relative strengths.

Then Swenson slipped on the ice going into Unalakleet, the first stop on the Bering Sea coast. Swenson hobbled through the rest of the race on an ankle that swelled so much he couldn't tie his boot. As Swenson tells it, when the two racers reached Elim, about 150 miles from Nome, "Emmitt came over. He couldn't find his dog food. I gave him a box of lamb chops. That's when he told me about this fancy belt buckle they were going to give for first place. For some reason that caught my imagination."

After a short break, they took off again. Swenson had a special light sled for the rest of the run into Nome. It had no brake.

As he chased Peters out of Elim, Swenson could see him once in a while on a hill ahead. The two teams eventually came to a high hill. "He kind of took off, running up the hill," Swenson explained. "I had that gimpy ankle and couldn't run. The trail ran along the side of the hill and my ankle was on the downhill side. We got to the top and it was hard packed."

That made the going slippery. With his sled missing a brake and his ankle injured, Swenson looked at the steep slope of the hill. His team went straight down. On that downhill run, Andy not only kept the team going, but he wove through a series of willow thickets so perfectly that the team missed everything safely and came out at the bottom ready to race.

Peters and Swenson reached White Mountain, seventy-seven miles from Nome, within minutes of each other. "We stayed about four hours and then got ready to leave. I looked down and there was a bolt missing from the sled where the stanchion met the runner. Emmitt took off. I had to hunt for a bolt. I lost about five minutes." Then Andy took off after the team in front. The two teams raced toward Safety, just twenty-two miles from Nome. Swenson was planning his move.

"I had to wait until just before Safety. If I could get ahead of him a little and get in and out of there cleanly, and he had trouble, we'd have it. I had faith Andy would go. The closer you got to the finish line, he wouldn't slack up — he'd just go harder."

Just outside of Safety, Andy pulled the team past his rivals. Swenson's team reached the checkpoint about one hundred feet in front, but it was enough. Checking in and out within a minute, Swenson and Andy raced toward Nome, gradually building their lead. Over the next twenty-two miles, they extended their lead until they crossed the finish line forty-two minutes ahead of Peters, and became the first dog and musher to win the Iditarod twice.

Over the course of his career from 1977 to 1983, Andy led Swenson's team to four Iditarod victories plus that close second-place finish, unprecedented at the time. That added up to about 8,400 miles under race pressure, not counting the shorter races and training trails.

Swenson retired Andy in 1984, but Andy did run one more race. Swenson loaned his favorite lead dog to friend Sonny Lindner for the inaugural running of the Yukon Quest, another thousand-mile race, this one from Fairbanks to Whitehorse in the Yukon. Though Andy ran in the team more than in the lead, several other drivers said that when they saw Andy on Lindner's team, they figured they'd already lost the race. Lindner won that race with Andy running the entire way at the age of nine.

Before the Iditarod that year, Swenson gave an emotional speech. He described packing for the race and leaving behind one dog, a dog who jumped up eagerly from his bed in the garage, ready for another try at the trail. Swenson lamented having to leave that dog behind. Though he never said the dog's name, everyone in that audience of maybe 300 people knew that it was Andy.

THE SHOE

Raised and trained by Syd Shaw in Sydney, Australia, an all black greyhound named The Shoe set records in the 1960s that reportedly still stand today. The Shoe was the son of two famous Australian greyhounds and began his racing career at the age of twenty months. During his first year of racing, beginning in 1967, The Shoe ran twenty-eight races. He won fourteen, finishing second six times and third four times. By the end of the year, racing at Australia's Harold Park, he was challenging the speed record for 500 yards. He tied the record of 26.2 seconds on November 4 and ran it in 26.3 seconds on December 2. On December 23, he broke the record, running the 500 yards in 26 seconds flat. The next spring, timers clocked The Shoe at 41.72 miles per hour, running 410 yards in 20.1 seconds. They estimated he ran the last hundred yards in 4.5 seconds, a speed of 45.45 miles per hour. It was the fastest time ever recorded for a greyhound.

> In 1968 an Australian greyhound was clocked as the fastest dog on earth ...

Becky Thatcher *Dalmatian*

BECKY THATCHER

From its earliest history, the Dalmatian has served man and horse as companion, hunter, and protector, but the breed is best known for working with firefighters. What painting of a nineteenth-century firehouse doesn't include a black-spotted white dog standing alert, ready to answer the alarm?

The Dalmatian's role as a firehouse dog grew out of its centuries-old tradition of working with horses. Dalmatian-like dogs were bred by the Ancient Greeks and, even before that, in Bengal in India, where they were used for hunting hares. Modern history first finds them associated with the Gypsies. Taking their name from the Dalmatia region on the Gulf of Venice in the former Yugoslavia, the dogs followed the horses of the Romany Gypsies through Europe. Eventually the handsome dogs attracted the attention of the nobility and joined the coaches of wealthy people moving from capital to capital. No European noble's coach was complete without a Dalmatian trotting along with the horses or riding on the driver's box.

> Dalmatians have a 200-year-old heritage as the friends and helpers of firefighters.

Among their duties, the dogs served to chase wolves away from the horses, herd errant domestic animals out of the road, even chase away a bandit or two.

As Europeans moved to the New World, Dalmatians came with them, still in their role as coach dogs. With the rise of cities came the need for organized fire-fighting companies. Early on, men pulled the fire department "pumpers" (small trucks equipped with pumps). As the cities grew and distances to fires became longer, firefighters turned to horses to pull the pumps quickly through the city streets. Along with the horses came the Dalmatian, as companion, guide, and sometimes heroic fire dog. The first of the Dalmatian fire dogs appears to have joined a brigade in Boston in the early 1800s. From there they spread along the East Coast and followed the migration west across the country. Many wealthy people who kept Dalmatians as coach dogs would donate a pup to their local fire department.

Pictures from this period often show a horse-drawn fire pumper racing to a fire, with a

Dog Heroes

black-and-white-spotted Dalmatian pacing the horses. The dog's natural disposition made him a friend to the fire-fighting men as well. Many firehouse dogs followed their masters into burning buildings, where they gave moral support and helped search for victims.

Hundreds of stories about heroic Dalmatians exist. One of the most striking involves a fire dog named Smoke. The dog arrived as a pup at Hook and Ladder Company Number 12 in New York City in the early twentieth century. Smoke was a direct descendent of a Dalmatian named Oakie who had been presented to the New York Fire Department by Cornelius Vanderbilt.

Within a year Smoke grew from an awkward pup into a dedicated fire dog. At the firehouse there was a specific series of rings for each of the New York companies. Smoke could distinguish his company's call from the others. When the fire bell rang for Company No. 12, Smoke would rise, ready to run out with the fire pumps. If the ring wasn't for his brigade, he'd curl up and go back to sleep.

Smoke's favorite companions were the gray draft horses stabled at the house to pull the fire equipment. He lived, though, during the time when fire fighting was becoming more mechanized, and he witnessed the change from horse-drawn pumps to engine-powered trucks. Reports from the time indicate that Smoke pined for his lost companions, but in time adjusted and ran with the trucks as he once had run with the horses.

Then one day in May of 1917, Smoke answered the alarm with his crew. Racing ahead of the truck, he charged to the scene of a fire raging though a chemical plant. Some of the firefighters already at the scene had succumbed to chlorine gas fumes emanating from the flaming building. Though his sensitive nose must have warned him against it, Smoke joined the men in the building. Everywhere firefighters were suffering from the deadly gas. Once, twice, and once again Smoke entered the building, leading firefighters to their comrades who had become overcome by the gas and lost consciousness.

After his third venture into the building, Smoke staggered out to the street, where he collapsed on the pavement. Men from his own company found him and put him in the captain's vehicle for a ride back to the firehouse. The next day, the normally friendly Smoke was a changed dog. The chlorine gas had affected his brain, and he began to growl at even his closest friends. The firefighters raised every cent they could to treat the dog, but the damage to his brain was too great. In order to ease his suffering, much to the sadness of all the men of Company 12, the faithful Dalmatian was put to sleep.

Once horses were no longer used in fire fighting, the Dalmatian wasn't needed as much in the firehouses. The dogs became pets and mascots, often accompanying a fire engine during a parade. Over the years they never lost their association with fire fighting and they continue to be a symbol of the profession.

Today some Dalmatians work with fire fighters

in a new way — by helping to educate human beings about fire prevention. One example is a Dalmatian named Becky Thatcher who lived in Springfield, Missouri. Wearing a bandanna with the insignia of the Springfield Fire Department, Becky the Fire Dog visited schools and organizations, serving as a symbol for fire safety.

Carefully trained by her master, Becky performed tricks to complement the talks given by firefighters. While children watched Becky's antics, they learned about fire safety. A favorite lesson among the children was what to do when someone's clothing catches fire. As the lecturer taught the children to "stop, drop, and roll," Becky would stand still, drop to her belly, then roll over. According to a letter from one grateful parent, Becky's lessons helped save the life of one child whose clothes were aflame. Doubtless the lessons taught by Becky and other fire education dogs have saved many other lives as well.

BRANDY

As terrorism became more common in the second half of the twentieth century, authorities searched for better methods to detect bombs aboard airplanes. While some machines had been developed to do the job, they were expensive and difficult to move. By the early 1970s, a few agencies had begun experimenting with dogs, but it wasn't until a German shepherd named Brandy demonstrated bomb-sniffing success that the use of dogs became universal. In 1972, shortly after a TWA airliner had taken off from New York for Los Angeles, a caller informed the airline that a bomb had been placed on board. The airplane turned around and returned to John F. Kennedy Airport. An officer led Brandy to the grounded aircraft and let the dog go to work. Brandy found the bomb just twelve minutes before it was set to explode, giving bomb experts enough time to defuse it. Brandy's success led the federal Law Enforcement Assistance Administration to fund a program to place trained bomb-sniffing dogs in airports throughout the United States. Today an airplane is supposedly never more than a half-hour away from an airport with a bomb-sniffing dog. The agency's statistics indicate that the trained dogs locate hidden explosives 96.6 percent of the time, in an average of sixteen minutes.

Bomb-sniffing dogs: why no airport should be without one ...

80

Winston *Yellow Labrador*

WINSTON

As dog heroes go, Winston Simmerdown almost didn't make it.

A pedigreed yellow Labrador retriever, Winston's line could be traced back six generations. At birth he showed all the promise of a show dog. However, Winston's first two owners gave up on him after he tore up furniture and gardens, clothes and shoes. He was passed on to field trainers, who tried to make him into a hunting dog. Their harsh training tactics took a lively dog and made him depressed and listless. Eventually Winston wound up at what might have been the kennel of last resort.

At that kennel, trainer Tony Bairos saw a dog who was energetic but distrustful and overemotional, who would throw himself against the chain-link fence of his kennel when he was upset. At first Bairos thought Winston might only be good for stud, but he gave the dog one more chance. Experienced at training dogs to find contraband drugs, Bairos started working with Winston. Before any drug-sniffing could begin, he had to gain the dog's confidence. After hours of walking and playing with the dog, the trainer taught Winston to retrieve a rolled-up towel. Over time, he added the scent of first marijuana, then other drugs, to the towel. Winston's reward for finding the towel was a game of tug-of-war with a section of fire hose — about the only thing the dog couldn't tear apart. As their work progressed, Bairos hid the towel in more and more difficult places until he was sure Winston was ready to work with narcotics officers.

> Considered a failure for much of his early life, this yellow Lab grew up to be a champion drug-sniffing dog.

About the time Winston reached the peak of his training, a citizen's group in Orange County, California, joined the sheriff's office in the war on drugs by purchasing Winston and paying for his training. The dog was paired up with Don Lambert, a fifteen-year veteran of police work. Because of his attachment to Bairos, it took Winston some time to accept Lambert as his new partner. But once they formed a bond and completed a drug-detection course together, Winston and Lambert became one of the most effective weapons against drug traffic that Southern California would ever see.

Over their nine-year partnership from 1982 to 1990, Winston and Lambert accounted for the prosecution of some 1,300 people involved in the drug trade. One judge said of Winston: "He has more credibility with me than most of the witnesses that appear before me."

In 1982 the idea of drug-sniffing dogs was relatively new. Only two other dogs were reported working in California at the time. As the use of dogs grew, drug dealers took to disguising the scent of their stashes with coffee, pepper, mothballs, garlic, even Vicks Vaporub.

It was no use. Winston couldn't be fooled. In one noted case, Lambert took Winston into a suspect house to search for drugs. The dealers had scattered mothballs throughout the house and even packed their drugs in a sealed, cedar-lined footlocker. Despite all the masking odors, Winston alerted on the footlocker within minutes. Inside, the police found 4,000 pounds of cocaine and $2.8 million in cash. At another time, Winston detected two pounds of cocaine that had been sealed in Mason jars, then hidden in a strongbox, which was taped above the rear axle of a car. Throughout his career, Winston also found drugs hidden in briefcases, cars, scuba tanks, aerosol cans, and all kinds of secret compartments in cars, homes, and boats.

Winston also could find money handled by drug dealers. Apparently American paper money absorbs odors from the fingers of people who touch it. So if someone has contact with drugs, the money they touch also will carry the scent of the drugs. In the largest bust to Winston's credit, local and federal agents raided a hotel room in Anaheim, California. Winston was brought in to help them search. He quickly led the agents to suitcases and boxes that contained more than $4 million in drug money.

Though it wasn't part of his job description, in one incident Winston saved his partner from serious injury, if not death. While Lambert and Winston worked their part of a drug bust in a parking lot, agents burst into a condominium nearby. A large man dove through a window from the second story and landed on a patio. He charged Lambert, throwing a punch as he came. Lambert ducked. Before he could recover, Winston had driven his full ninety pounds into the man's chest, knocked him to the ground and sinking his teeth into a leg.

Winston's talents went beyond sniffing out drugs and money. As his fame grew, he became a lecturer of sorts, visiting school classrooms with Lambert and carrying the anti-drug message. As Lambert told schoolchildren about the dangers of drug use, Winston demonstrated his abilities and helped to excite the children about the fight against drug traffic.

Winston wasn't only famous with children. Criminals knew about him, too. Police learned that several drug traffickers put a price on Winston's head, one of them for $50,000.

In his nine-year career, Winston was credited

BARCO

During the early 1980s, agents of the U.S. Border Patrol took to calling the southeastern Texas border with Mexico "Cocaine Alley" because it had become a gateway for illegal drugs entering the United States. To intercept the tons of narcotics being smuggled in, the Border Patrol enlisted the help of drug-sniffing dogs. One of their first was a Belgian Malinois-Airedale cross named Barco. On their first day of duty, April 9, 1987, Barco and his partner Rocky located 131 pounds of marijuana spread through nine different vehicles and valued at $104,800. Either on a leash or roaming free, the dogs would be led by a handler to a suspect vehicle. If the dog smelled drugs, he would signal by sitting down, giving the Border Patrol agents legal probable cause to search the vehicle. By the end of 1992, Barco had participated in investigations of 466 cases and identified more than thirty-three tons of marijuana and cocaine. The street value of Barco's finds came to more than $181 million. But Barco's heroism didn't stop there. In July of 1987, when the roof of a Brownsville department store collapsed, Border Patrol dogs were brought in to help find survivors in the rubble. The dogs, including Barco, located fourteen persons trapped in the tons of concrete and steel, saving six of them from death. Sixteen hours into the operation, Barco alerted on a specific spot in the wreckage. It took rescue workers hours to extract the eight-year-old girl Barco had found. Denise Carrera was the last person rescued, and Barco was personally credited with saving her life.

Law enforcement dogs across the country save lives in many different ways ...

with finding more than $44 million worth of illegal drugs and another $34.5 million in drug-related cash, bringing the cash value of his contribution to the fight against drugs to almost $80 million. On top of that, Winston helped police seize the property of convicted drug dealers, including cars, houses, boats, and other possessions worth another $8 million ... all because of a dog who almost didn't make it.

83

Granite *Husky*

GRANITE

Through the history of sled dog racing, there have been mushers who dominated the sport: Leonhard Seppala, Emil St. Godard, George Attla, Roland Lombard, Rick Swenson, Susan Butcher. While these drivers are highly respected for their ability to train and race dogs, it's also acknowledged that much of their success usually can be traced to a single dog, a leader who had something extra, a dog who led the team to victory time after time.

Such a dog was Granite, an Alaskan husky who was the leader of Susan Butcher's team in Alaska's Iditarod Trail Sled Dog Race. Though unusually shy for a lead dog, Granite was fantastically fast and unswervingly obedient. He and his partner Tekla were a once-in-a-lifetime team. While Granite kept the team moving at a competitive speed, maybe eleven or twelve miles per hour, and took the commands to turn, Tekla would demonstrate an uncanny memory for following trail, finding checkpoints, even remembering where the dogs stayed in the villages during previous races.

For leaders and the other dogs in a twelve- to eighteen-member team, the primary job is racing. But over more than a thousand miles of winter trail through the Alaska wilderness, dog teams often come up against rougher challenges than simply beating the other teams. They face the toughest conditions the Alaska winter can throw at them: howling blizzards ... frozen rivers with water running over the top of the ice ... mountain ranges up to 3,400 feet above sea level ... temperatures dropping to −50° F and below ... even attacks by wild animals.

When the elements gather against them, the sled dogs, and in particular the lead dogs, become more than racing machines. They have to rise to meet the challenge, at times bringing their team and their driver out of danger. Sometimes mushers have to trust their dogs to find a way out of trouble. Susan

> The lead dog of Iditarod champion Susan Butcher, Granite saved the team twice from dangers on the trail.

85

Butcher gave Granite that kind of trust.

During the 1984 Iditarod, Butcher chased the leaders out of Unalakleet, where the Iditarod Trail first meets the ice of the Bering Sea. Moving north along the coast on an unseasonably warm day, the dogs followed the trail out onto the ice across Shaktoolik Lagoon, toward the village of the same name. Partway across and several hundred yards from shore, the ice began to move, some slabs rocking ever so gently from side to side.

Butcher called "haw" for Granite to turn to his left, toward the solid ground on a narrow strip of beach. Though it took him off the trail he'd been following, with its lingering scent from previous teams and the hard-packed snow that sled dogs prefer, Granite swung to his left and the team followed. Behind them the ice began cracking, then rolling in waves. Granite ran for shore, dragging the other dogs, the sled, and Butcher toward safety. Almost as Granite reached shore, the ice collapsed under the sled, twenty or thirty feet behind him. Butcher, standing on the runners, went into the water. Granite kept chugging toward shore, finally pulling the team and sled up onto the hard ground on the beach. Safe there, Butcher and her dogs continued north, still in the competition in the race for Nome.

Successful mushers have a rapport with their dogs that can seem almost extrasensory. All through the race, they watch their dogs carefully. Each dog has his own signals — a head up, a tail down, ears up, ears back, ears down — that all tell the driver something.

Her dogs' signals were the first indication Butcher had of trouble during the 1985 race as she crossed the lowlands of the Susitna and Skwenta River valleys. As each pair of dogs disappeared over a small rise in front of her, their ears perked up. Butcher knew something was happening down the trail.

By the time Butcher and the sled came over the rise, her lead dogs were being attacked by an angry cow moose. It was not an uncommon experience. Moose don't like to get out of the way, leaving the hard-packed trail for the deeper snow around it; also, some moose probably perceive a dog team as a pack of wolves. Whatever the reason, the moose stomped and kicked her way through the dogs.

The dogs, restrained by their traces, could not get away. Butcher later recalled most of the dogs lying flat, "trying to melt into the snow." Granite reacted differently. He attacked the moose. According to Butcher, he jumped to the rescue, fighting for her and the rest of the team. Then the moose's attack stopped. Butcher took off her parka and waved it in the animal's face, trying to scare it away. The moose charged again, kicking at the dogs. Almost as quickly, the moose backed off, appearing to calm down. Butcher thought the attack was finally over.

It started again. The moose charged into the dogs. This time the moose passed Granite and got between him and some of the dogs farther back in the team. Granite rose to the rescue, snapping and biting the moose's hind legs. The moose, kicking

86

wildly, caught the dog in the head, hurling him against a tree.

Another sled dog team came up from behind them, and the driver was carrying a firearm. Once he'd realized the situation, the driver killed the moose, saving Butcher and the rest of her dogs. With the battle finally over, Butcher was relieved until she began assessing the damage. Two dogs had been killed by the attack. Eleven others suffered some sort of injury. Butcher was out of the race, but she and Granite would return another year. Through the late 1980s, with Granite in lead, Butcher won four Iditarods, three of them in a row.

BRIDGET

Late in March of 1982, despite a heavy snowstorm in California's Sierra Mountains, Anna Conrad skied to her job as a lift operator at Alpine Meadows ski area. When she arrived, the area manager bawled her out for taking a chance in the mountains during avalanche season. Minutes later the lesson slid horribly home as an avalanche roared down the mountain and through the ski center. Conrad was thrown to the floor of a locker room. Wall lockers crashed over her but landed on a bench, leaving her with a little air to breathe. Trapped beneath fifteen feet of snow and the debris of the lodge, Conrad ate snow to survive while searchers worked over her head. Hampered by new snow, rescue workers searched for three days using dogs from the Wilderness Finders, a California search and rescue team nicknamed WOOF. A German shepherd named Bridget snuffled through the wreckage until she alerted right over Conrad. Despite Conrad's cries for help, the searchers didn't find her. Two days later, in clear weather, Bridget returned to the spot. This time workers began to dig there, carefully cutting away timbers with chain saws. Several times they lowered Bridget into the hole for an indication of which way to dig. Eventually they reached Conrad and lifted her out. Though she lost both of her feet to the cold, Conrad survived. She was the only survivor of the avalanche. It was the first time reported in North America that a search and rescue dog had found a live avalanche victim.

When all the world has given up on you, count on a dog to come to your rescue ...

87

88

McCafferty *Golden retriever*

MCCAFFERTY

Each of the dogs in this book was chosen for some act or a lifetime of action that made them stand out from the norm. But what about everybody's dog — our companion, our playmate, the puppy who chews our shoes? After all, few of us have had our lives changed by the work of an outstandingly heroic dog, but most of us have been touched by the simple love of a dog who became part of the family.

Mike Wigger lived alone in Fairbanks, Alaska, in an apartment too small for a dog. His desire for a dog was so strong he read books on breeds and training so that when the time came he could find the right dog and train it properly. He eventually convinced his landlord to allow him to keep a dog, but it had to stay outside. Wigger built a kennel and went in search of a dog.

A heavy equipment operator, Wigger was digging a basement for a residence in Fairbanks when the owner told him of a litter of golden retrievers that had been born in the neighborhood. Wigger already had decided to get a golden, and he went to the family to see the dogs. "I read a pretty thorough book on training. I knew how to spot a good dog," he said. He took a rubber ball with him and played with the pups. "McCafferty was the only one who seemed to do things on her own," he said.

From that day on, Mike Wigger and J.J. McCafferty, as she was known to the American Kennel Club, were inseparable friends. Wigger spent hundreds of hours training his new dog. She learned to obey the commands "sit," "stay," "come," "lay down," and others. The two friends went everywhere together, walking as much as three miles a day even in the cold weather of an Alaskan winter. "We wouldn't go out if it got to fifty or fifty-five below, but any other time," Wigger said. Later, as McCafferty grew older, he set the limit at twenty-five below zero.

Because they took their walks along a four-lane highway, Wigger taught McCafferty to wait for his

> For thirteen years, this beautiful golden retriever was one man's faithful companion and best friend.

command at places where the sidewalk met the street: "I was always afraid she'd get hit by a car. She didn't fear them, didn't know they could hurt her. I worked with her. She would sit at a light. I'd tell her to stay, and I'd walk across the street. I'd make her stay through a light change. Then, when it turned green again, I'd signal her to cross."

Besides voice commands, McCafferty learned to respond to hand signals and to a whistle. She would run a few hundred feet ahead of him and, when she turned to see where he was, he would guide her to her objective. At the sound of the whistle, McCafferty would sit down and wait for his command. "We got a little lax over the years. We trusted each other. We could look at each other and know what the other was thinking."

Wigger worked a gold mine near Fairbanks and that was their favorite place: "She was a miner's dog. You know how some dogs will take a stick and carry it around all day? Well, McCafferty would take a rock and do the same thing. She could wear your arm off throwing rocks for her. She wasn't crazy about it or anything, but she'd retrieve forever."

At the mine, McCafferty could amuse herself for hours. While the men worked the mine, McCafferty might spend all day digging out a ground squirrel or just watching the work. One of her favorite pastimes was watching the rocks tumble down the sluice boxes as the miners looked for pay. McCafferty would stick her nose in the water, pick out rocks, and drop them next to her. "At the end of the day, there'd be this little stack of McCafferty-

sized rocks. Her nose would be all black from the mud," Wigger said. Sometimes McCafferty would find other toys by digging around the mine. Over the years the dog unearthed several woolly mammoth bones and those of prehistoric horses and bison.

The miners used four-wheelers to get around the area. When Wigger set out, McCafferty had to jump up on the back and sit there, riding along like the queen of the tundra. "She was a lady all the way," Wigger said.

In all the thirteen years Wigger lived in that small apartment, McCafferty never spent a winter indoors. Wigger finally bought a house in early 1994. "I wanted her to be queen of the house," he said. Then, in the middle of a night in September, he heard her fall. Wigger took her to a veterinarian, who wanted to keep her "for observation." "I knew what he was saying but I couldn't leave her," Wigger said. "I took her to the mine and let her out. Her heart was willing, but the body was unable. When I got back to Fairbanks, I took her back to the vet. I knew she had to be put to sleep. I couldn't stay for it. I couldn't watch. Even still, I didn't realize the agony could be so strong."

According to Wigger, McCafferty made sure that he wouldn't be alone after her death. In his years of living by himself, he remained very close to his mother. When she died, he only had McCafferty. Then, in the summer of 1994, he met a woman named Patricia and they fell in love. Together they moved into the house where McCafferty was to spend her first winter indoors. When McCafferty died, Wigger decided that "it was a female conspiracy. They handed me from Mother to McCafferty to Patricia. I kind of felt, the way everything happened, McCafferty hung in there long enough to see that I was in good hands."

Wigger saved the ashes of his long-time friend and planned, come summer, to scatter them around the gold mine where the two of them had spent so many wonderful years together.

ROVER & FIDO

No book on dogs would be complete without at least mentioning, if not the two most popular dog names, at least the two biggest clichés. The name "Rover" can be traced to George Washington, who gave his own dog that name, popularizing it through at least two centuries. While the name "Fido" had been around a while, it wasn't until Abraham Lincoln reached the White House and his part-hound mongrel Fido became famous that the name joined "Rover" as the two standard names for pet dogs. Other famous White House dogs have included Warren G. Harding's Airedale, Laddie Boy; Franklin D. Roosevelt's black Scottish terrier, Fala; and George Bush's springer spaniel, Millie. As a vice presidential candidate in 1952, Richard Nixon mentioned his family's cocker spaniel, Checkers, in a speech that helped saved his political career. Lyndon B. Johnson had to face the wrath of dog lovers across America after he was photographed lifting his two beagles, Him and Her, up by the ears. President Johnson insisted that the dogs enjoyed it, and that their yelps were yelps of joy.

The powerful influence of the president, and his dog ...

🐾 DOG ALMANAC

A collection of facts, figures, and trivia about the canine world.

92

Humans began teaching dogs new tricks about 12,000 years ago when canines, descendants of wolves, became the first domesticated animals.

In the United States alone, there are more than 50 million dogs. They guide the blind, search for lost children, aid the police, hunt for wild game, protect families, and provide friendship.

Dogs cannot see as well as people or distinguish certain colors, but they have a fine-tuned sense of hearing that allows them to distinguish, for example, the sound of their owner's car. They recognize most objects by their sense of smell, and their ability to recognize the smell of certain compounds is millions of times more acute than that of humans.

The American Kennel Club lists 130 breeds of dog, each with its own features. The smallest is the Chihuahua, which normally weighs about four pounds. The biggest is the Saint Bernard, which can weigh as much as 200 pounds.

Most dogs are carried in the womb for about nine weeks before birth. A typical litter is from one to twelve puppies, depending on the breed.

Visit any home in America and there's a better than one-in-three chance that you will find a dog on the premises. Americans are more likely to own a dog than a cat, but because cat owners often have more than one feline, there are about 4.5 million more cats than dogs in U.S. households.

Oklahoma, where nearly half of the households have a dog, is the most dog-friendly state in the Union. The New England states have the lowest percentage of households with dogs.

The privileged class of America's dogs are those registered with the American Kennel Club. Top dogs in this category are Labrador retrievers, with 124,899 of them listed in 1993. The second most popular dog was the Rottweiler, with 104,160 registered, while German shepherds ranked third with 79,936. Rounding out the rest of the top ten, there were 75,882 cocker spaniels ... 68,125 golden retrievers ... 67,850 poodles ... 61,051 beagles ... 48,573 dachshunds ... 42,816 Dalmatians ... and 41,113 Shetland sheepdogs.

Those of us who can afford to pamper our pets often do so. There are about one hundred resorts for dogs in the United States, reports the *Wall Street Journal*. At one such kennel in the suburbs of Detroit, the dogs get swimming classes in a pond, appointments with the barber, food treats, and walks outside — all for eleven dollars a night.

Though one-fifth of New York City residents have dogs, some New Yorkers don't like to venture out on the streets with their dogs. That's why the new breed of personal dog walkers do not have to beg for business in the Big Apple. Pet walkers pick up a dog once a day and take it outside for a stroll around the block.

In China, where many people can't afford a dog of their own, there are those who cater to petless people who want to enjoy the thrill of walking the dog. In a suburb of Beijing, mutts from a stable known as the "Divine Land of Beloved Dogs" can be rented out on an hourly basis.

The most popular dogs among wealthy people in China include the Shih Tzu, which originated in China in ancient times, and the Pekinese, which can be traced back in China to the 700s. A pure-bred Pekinese in China costs the equivalent of fifty years' pay for a typical urban worker.

Dogs give unconditional love and give their owners a sense of purpose. A recent study by two California researchers revealed that people with dogs took more walks and reported less dissatisfaction with their personal lives.

— *Compiled by Dermot Cole*

Suggested Reading

Alexander, Charles. *Bobbie: A Great Collie*. New York: Dodd, Mead & Company, 1966.

Atkinson, Eleanor. *Greyfriars Bobby*. London: Puffin Books, 1962.

Beene, Richard. "Best Weapon in Drug War May Be Man's Best Friend." *Los Angeles Times*, March 3, 1990, Orange County edition.

Brey, Catherine F. and Lena F. Reed. *The New Complete Bloodhound*. New York: Howell Book House, 1991.

Brown, Beth. *Dogs That Work for a Living*. New York: Funk & Wagnalls, 1970.

Bruns, James, comp. *Owney: Mascot of the Railway Mail Service*. Washington, DC: National Postal Museum, Smithsonian Institution, 1992.

Carter, Gordon. *Dogs at Work*. New York: Abelard-Schuman, 1966.

Casey, Brigid and Wendy Haugh. *Sled Dogs*. New York: Dodd, Mead & Company, 1983.

Caulkins, Janet V. *Pets of the Presidents*. Brookfield, CT: The Millbrook Press, 1992.

Cellura, Dominique. *Travelers of the Cold: Sled Dogs of the Far North*. Anchorage: Alaska Northwest Books, 1990.

Chern, Margaret Booth. *The New Complete Newfoundland*. New York: Howell Book House, 1976.

Clemens, Virginia Phelps. *Superanimals and Their Unusual Careers*. Philadelphia: The Westminster Press, 1979.

Conniff, Richard. "We shed 50 million skin cells a day; they make good scents to a hound." *Smithsonian*, January 1986, 64-72.

Coolidge, W. A. B. *Alpine Studies*. London: Longmans, Green, 1912.

Curtis, Patricia. *Dogs on the Case: Search Dogs Who Help Save Lives*. New York: E. P. Dutton, 1989.

"Death of 'Smoke,' Fire-fighter." *Literary Digest*, June 2, 1917.

Deneberg, R. V. and Eric Seidman. *The Dog Catalog*. New York: Grosset & Dunlap, 1978.

"Dog lands lifeline, saves 92 on wreck." *New York Times*, December 17, 1919.

Downey, Fairfax. *Dogs for Defense: American Dogs in the Second World War*. New York: Trustees of Dogs for Defense, Inc., 1955.

Downey, Fairfax. *Dogs of Destiny*. New York: Charles Scribner's Sons, 1949.

Fichter, George S. *Working Dogs*. New York: Franklin Watts, 1979.

Fleming, Thomas. "Winston's Last Chance." *Reader's Digest*, November 1988, 100-104.

Francis, Cle. "Border Patrol's Star 'Sniffers' Lead Drug War." *Dog World*, July 1988.

Frank, Morris and Blake Clark. *First Lady of the Seeing Eye*. New York: Henry Holt and Company, 1957.

Handel, Leo A. *A Dog Named Duke: True Stories of German Shepherds at Work With the Law*. New York: J. P. Lippincott Company, 1966.

Hart, Audrey and Edward Hart. *Working Dogs*. London: B. T. Batsford Ltd., 1984.

Hartwell, Dickson. *Dogs Against Darkness: The Story of the Seeing Eye*. New York: Dodd, Mead & Company, 1942.

Hubbard, Clifford L. B. *Working Dogs of the World*. London: Sidgwick and Jackson Ltd., 1947.

Kay, Helen. *Man and Mastiff: The Story of the St. Bernard Dog*. New York: The Macmillian Company, 1967.

Knight, Eric. "Lassie Come Home." *Saturday Evening Post*, July-August 1977.

Krause, Carolyn. "The Firedog Connection." *Dog World*, August 1988, 20.

Linderman, Joan M. and Virginia Funk. *The Complete Akita*. New York: Howell Book House, 1983.

Lo Bello, Nina. "The Greatest Detective in Dogdom." *Reader's Digest*, August 1964, 57-60.

"Loyalty, Sagacity and Courage: The Heritage of Dogkind." *National Geographic*, March 1919, 253-275.

Marko, Katherine McGlade. *Animals in Orbit*. New York: Franklin Watts, 1991.

McCloy, James. *Dogs at Work*. New York: Crown Publishers, 1979.

McCoy, J. J. *Animal Servants of Man*. New York: Lothrop, Lee & Shepherd Company, 1963.

Newfoundland Club of America. *This is the Newfoundland*. Jersey City, NJ: T. F. C. Publications, Inc., 1971.

Olmert, Michael. "No one actually has canonized the St. Bernard." *Smithsonian*, March 1990, 71-81.

O'Neill, Catherine. *Dogs on Duty*. Washington, DC: The National Geographic Society, 1988.

Orbaan, Albert. *Dogs Against Crime*. New York: The John Day Company, 1968.

People's Dispensary for Sick Animals. *The PDSA Dickin Medal: The Animals' V. C.* Shropshire, England.

Putnam, Peter Brock. *Love in the Lead*. New York: E. P. Dutton, 1979.

"Rags, Dog Veteran of War, Is Dead at 20; Terrier That Lost Eye in Service is Honored." *New York Times*, March 22, 1936.

Rennick, Penny, ed. *Dogs of the North*. Anchorage: The Alaska Geographic Society, 1987.

Rohan, Jack. *Rags: The Story of a Dog Who Went to War*. New York: Harper & Brothers Publishers, 1930.

Sayer, Angela. *The Complete Book of the Dog*. New York: Multimedia Productions Ltd., 1985.

Schoder, Judith. *Canine Careers: Dogs at Work*. New York: Julian Messner, 1981.

Siegel, Mary Ellen and Hermine M. Koplin. *More Than a Friend: Dogs With a Purpose*. New York: Walker & Company, 1984.

Silverstein, Alvin, and Virginia Silverstein. *Dogs: All About Them*. New York: Lothrop, Lee & Shepherd Books, 1986.

Stevens, Paul Drew. *Real Animal Heroes*. New York: Sharp & Dunnigan Publications, 1988.

Sturgis, Kent. "Following Granite." *Alaska Magazine*, March 1988.

Treen, Alfred and Esmeralda Treen. *Dalmatian, Coach Dog, Firehouse Dog*. New York: Howell Book House, 1981.

Tremain, Ruthven. *The Animals' Who's Who*. New York: Charles Scribner's Sons, 1982.

Weatherwax, Rudd B. and John H. Rothwell. *The Story of Lassie*. New York: Duell, Sloan & Pearce, 1950.

Whitney, Leon F. "Amazing Feats of Bloodhounds." *Popular Science Monthly*, July 1935, 24-5.

Wood, Gerald L. *The Guinness Book of Pet Records*. Middlesex, England: Guinness Books, 1984.

Tim Jones and Boone

About the Author

An Alaskan since 1973, Tim Jones is a former newspaper and magazine editor who left behind the confines of a more urban life in Anchorage in 1980. He has been a boat captain in Alaska's Prince William Sound and built homes in the Bush and in Valdez. He has edited several books, and his articles have appeared in numerous magazines.

Jones's books include the enduring best-seller, *The Last Great Race,* about the Iditarod Trail Sled Dog Race, published by Madrona Publishers and Stackpole Books. His other titles include: *Race Across Alaska* (Stackpole Books, co-authored with Libby Riddles), *Wild Critters* (Epicenter Press and Graphic Arts Center Publishing Co.), and *More Wild Critters* (Graphic Arts Center Publishing Co.).

In addition to his writing, Jones monitors oil-spill drills and training for a citizens' group established in the wake of the *Exxon Valdez* oil spill to advise the oil industry in Prince William Sound. He and his wife Barbara, son Justin, and daughter Ariel share time between Valdez and Talkeetna, Alaska.

About the Artist

Jon Van Zyle is an internationally recognized wildlife artist living with his wife, Charlotte, in Eagle River, Alaska, where he paints in a studio attached to his log home. He is also known for his paintings of northern landscapes, wolves, dog-mushing, and village life in Alaska.

"I grew up in a family where art and animals — especially dogs — were all-important," Van Zyle recalls. "My mother raised dogs for a living."

Van Zyle has a team of Siberian huskies, and twice has run the Iditarod Trail Sled Dog Race in Alaska. His work is featured in *Best of Alaska,* an artbook co-published by Epicenter Press and Graphic Arts Center Publishing Co. Other books illustrated by Van Zyle include *Iditarod Classics* (Epicenter Press), *Eyes of Gray Wolf* and *Honey Paw and Lightfoot* (both from Chronicle Books), and *Caribou Journey* (Little, Brown & Co.).

Jon Van Zyle and Sparky